THE MAR.

© 2014 Michael Marcovici

ISBN 9783735737250

„Herstellung und Verlag: BoD – Books on Demand, Norderstedt"

Bibliografische Information der Deutschen Nationalbibliothek: Die Deutsche Nationalbibliothek verzeichnet diese Publikation in der Deutschen Nationalbibliografie; detaillierte bibliografische Daten sind im Internet über **www.dnb.de** abrufbar.

CONTENTS

THE MARKETING BIBLE

Some form of primitive marketing existed the first time one of our prehistoric ancestors bartered a flint for a piece of food but, obviously, we have become a lot more sophisticated since then.

The science of marketing, if we can call it that, probably started in the 1950s with Philip Kotler but it really began to gain more widespread acceptance and use in the 60s and 70s. Now it is a major and indispensable business discipline made only the stronger by the advent of the internet.

Marketing has always comprised lots of different facets and probably means different things to different people. Some people see it as sales, others as advertising, others as market research and some as business management or strategy. All of these have their part to play in marketing but the discipline relies on the integration and interplay of all these elements – and more – to produce desired outcomes.

A marketing oriented business has to understand the importance of research, planning and analysis; realise whom their target audience is, what characteristics define them and what sort of product offers and messages they are likely to respond to. But marketers also have to understand the nuts and bolts of the techniques of getting goods to market, creating demand for the goods, building image and awareness and aftersales service. Layered over all of this is the critical understanding of the financial and budgetary aspects of marketing. It is no use selling millions of units at a price where each unit loses money or spending budget on an ad campaign that generates less than it costs. All of these factors have to be carefully calculated and weighed in order to produce coherent and effective marketing.

This compilation looks at all the varied aspects of marketing that make up the whole of this crucial and , sometimes, complex discipline. From basic principles through to some of the more detailed aspects of research, online marketing and media this opens the gateway to effective marketing in your business and could start you on the road to success – or push you further along if you are already on the journey.

Happy marketing.

1

THE HISTORY OF MARKETING

A brief history of marketing

In some ways marketing is as old as civilization itself. You may have seen films based in ancient Greece or Rome with images of bustling market stalls and traders actively engaged in persuasive communications. Of course these traders would not have called their activities marketing and their activities may seem far removed from someone ordering airline tickets via a website.

The concept of marketing that we now see has more to do with developments during the industrial revolution of the 18th and 19th centuries. This was a period of rapid social change driven by technological and scientific innovation (see BBC history website). One result was that for the first time the production of goods was separated from their consumption. Mass production, developing transport infrastructure and growing mass media meant that producers needed to, and could develop more sophisticated ways of managing the distribution of goods.

The production orientation era

For much of the industrial revolution goods were generally scarce and producers could sell pretty much all that they could produce, as long as people could afford to buy them. Their focus was therefore on production and distribution at the lowest possible cost and what marketing management that there was considered these issues (for example, reducing distribution costs, opening new markets).

The sales orientation era

From the start of the twentieth century to the period following the Second World War (although the development was interrupted by the wars) competition grew and the focus of marketing turned to selling. Communications, advertising and branding started to become more important (see archive at the History of Advertising Trust website) as companies needed to sell the increasing outputs of production in an increasingly crowded market. Marketing was therefore still a 'slave' to production, but focussed on distribution, communication and persuading customers that one manufacturer's goods were better than another's.

The marketing orientation era

From the 1960s onwards most markets have become saturated (the size of the market remains the same). This means that there is now intense competition for customers. The sophistication of marketing management has therefore developed into what we now see in a modern marketing department. Marketers are involved at a strategic level within the organisation and therefore inform an organisation about what should be produced, where it should be sold, how much should be charged for it and how it should be communicated to consumers. Modern marketers research markets and consumers. They attempt to understand consumer needs (and potential needs) and allocate organisational resources appropriately to meet these needs. Modern marketers are particularly interested in brands. They are also increasingly interested in ensuring that employees understand marketing, i.e. that everyone within the organisation involves themselves with marketing activities.

So what might you take from this very brief historical perspective?

Firstly, consider that marketing started as an inward looking discipline – focussing on what the organisation produced. Now marketing is outward looking. It brings an understanding of markets and of consumers into the organisation.

Secondly, you might consider that the marketing that you are familiar with today is, in fact, a very recent development – marketing is still a very new subject. You might also note that although we can talk about a 'marketing orientation', many organisations – especially small and medium enterprise – act as though they are still in the period of production or sales orientation. In the absence of a good understanding of marketing, organisations may still focus on production or sales.

Thirdly, modern definitions of marketing hide the fact that the development of modern marketing management has not been a coordinated process. Origins in production and managing distribution mean that manufacturers have been quicker to adopt marketing practice than, say, the service sector, including banks and much of the tourism industry.

Finally you might consider that marketing has changed rapidly over this century and it continues to change. The sorts of activities that you might be involved with at the end of your marketing career might be very different from the marketing we see today. As a professional marketer you should be particularly sensitive to changes in society, technology, and the world economy.

If you are interested in history, the Zenithmedia timeline provides a good overview of the major media developments that have influenced marketing

http://media3.bournemouth.ac.uk/ marketing/02defining/01history.html

WHY HAS MARKETING CHANGED OVER THE YEARS?

Global Administrator

Marketing has gone through rapid changes these past five to ten years, and it's definitely not slowing down anytime soon. These past years of trying to acquire prospects, leads, and customers is beginning to get more and more difficult. Simply placing ads in the local newspaper or yellow pages doesn't bring in the same business that it once did. The major shift of marketing has moved to the internet. Even though the internet is nothing new, it's now become one of the best ways to attract potential customers and clients.

A major reason that marketing techniques are changing so fast is due to the fact that the internet and technology are constantly improving. With the majority of your potential clients having access to high speed internet, search engines and online video sites; consumers can quickly learn the product's information from the comfort of their home or office. Websites like Facebook and Twitter are a great way to connect with your target audience and keep those relationships going. Blogging is also a great way to express ideas or products and to keep your business in the minds of your customers.

Marketing techniques are also changing because of the shift in which people communicate nowadays. Between text messaging and video conferencing, the need to set up a lunch meeting is becoming obsolete (As for the need to travel across the country to meet with someone face to face is also beginning to be viewed as a waste of money). Video conferencing has come a long way. With the combination of high speed internet connections and great conferencing websites, the technology is in place for people to feel like the person is in the room with them when they're really on the other side of the country.

Consumers today have more choices than ever before. Unless you own a large franchise, offering products at a super cheap price probably won't work for you. So instead of selling your products dirt cheap, focus on customer service and the quality of the product you are selling. Always remember that a comparable alternative is only a few mouse clicks away. That is why using the internet to market your business is more important than ever before. It's cheap and can be seen by virtually everyone you would like it to.

http://www.ibank.com/iBank-Blog/December-2011/Why-has-marketing-changed-over-the-years

2

<u>What Marketing Means</u> <u>Today</u>

What Can We Expect From The Next Decade Of Marketing?

It's been nearly half a century since Philip Kotler first published his Principles of Marketing, which has defined the practice of millions of professionals worldwide ever since. It's no stretch to say that before Kotler, there was no true marketing profession.

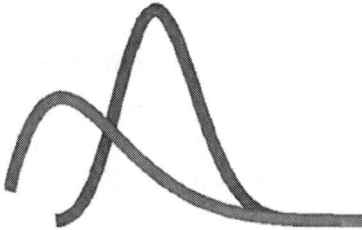

What made Kotler different than what came before is that he took insights from other fields, such as economics, social science and analytics and applied them to the marketing arena. Although that may seem basic now, it was groundbreaking then.

Today technology is transforming marketing once again. Although up to this point, most of the impact has been tactical, over the next decade or so there will be a major strategic transformation. This, of course, will be a much harder task because we will not only have to change what we do, but how we think and many will be left behind. Here's a short guide.

From Messages to Experiences

In the 20th century, promotion dominated the field of marketing. While evaluating opportunities was important, advertising, especially on TV, was what drove budgets and, as a result, strategic thinking. Not surprisingly, coming up with the right message and broadcasting to the right people at the right time was of paramount importance.

Today, however, digital technology has enabled us to retarget consumers when they respond to a message and that has changed marketing forever. In effect, we must make the shift from grabbing attention to holding attention.

That means that brands will have to learn to be more like publishers and develop content skills. It also means that marketers will have to create a genuine value exchange rather than just coming up with catchy ad slogans and price promotions. Like it or not, we've entered a post-promotional paradigm.

From Rational Benefits to The Passion Economy

In the past, we focused on rational benefits to entice consumers to support our brands. Show that you are better in a clear, rational way and, so the thinking went, you could build a loyal following.

However, we're not rational, calculating machines, but emotional driven creatures who are subject to an whole array of cognitive biases and new research has changed the psychology of marketing. For example, research shows that while a price promotion may spurs sales, it lessens enjoyment and can hurt the brand long-term.

In effect, it's become clear that we are not operating in a rational economy, but a passion economy, where a sense of purpose determines how people will act and brand associations, rather than brand attributes, determine marketing success. So we'll have to learn to focus on share of synapse as well as share of market.

From Strategic Planning to Adaptive Strategy

Marketing strategy has always been numbers driven. We survey a small selection of the population and then scale up those samples to make decisions. Unfortunately, our numbers are always wrong. They are backward looking, fraught with data. As the Web of Things becomes more pervasive, this will allow us to truly co-create with our consumers.

In effect, by increasing our failures in the virtual world, we can improve our performance in the real one.

From Brands to Platforms

For most of the 20th century, businesses focused on developing proprietary value chains. As they became more successful and added scale, theircompetitive advantage would grow in terms of quality, efficiency and brand equity. Brands were, in effect, just another asset to be accounted for and then leveraged.

Digital technology is forcing marketers to rethink their historical approach to marketing. We are no longer operating in a scale economy, but in a semantic economy where the connectivity drives value and brands are becoming open platforms and ecosystems rather than assets to be closed off and protected.

This has already become clear in technology products, where API's and SDK's have become standard, but asthe world of bits invades the world of atoms, all marketers will need to connect in order to survive.

So, while Kotler reconciled marketing with the standards of business, over the next decade we will have to reconcile marketing with the standards of technology and, as Martin Heidegger once argued, technology isn't important because of what it builds, but because of what it uncovers.

What Do We Mean When We Say Marketing?

Heidi Cohen

12 Marketing Elements

To help us understand what marketing means in today's evolving media environment, where increasingly connected prospects, customers and the public interact with a broad range of businesses, seventy-two senior marketing executives were asked to define their profession. Of course any large collection of marketing definitions is sure to yield a diverse set of responses. It's like the group of blind men describing an elephant where each speaks of just that part of the elephant they're touching at the moment.

Simply put, Dr. Phillip Kotler defined marketing as "the science and art of exploring, creating, and delivering value to satisfy the needs of a target market at a profit."

12 Marketing elements

Here are twelve consistent marketing elements that ran across these seventy-two seemingly divergent marketing definitions.

1. Know your customer. Segment your target market to identify their pain points according to Joe Pulizzi. For Humphrey Rolleston, marketing is about developing deep insights into customer behavior and overall market conditions. This helps you to create marketing personas.

2. Develop the right product. David Meerman Scott says to create valuable products especially for your customers that solve their problems. For Jeanniey Mullen, if you've targeted your audience properly, they'll become addicted to your products and services. As Ken Rosen puts it: offer stuff your customers crave.

3. Meet customers' needs. The challenge is that consumers may not always be sure of what they need and where they're willing to make their tradeoffs. In Doreen Moran'swords, marketing helps customers understand how much they need something they never knew they needed. Marketing delivers products that prospects want more efficiently and effectively than the competition, according to Paul Kulavis. (Note: This was the only mention of competition.)

4. Develop and distribute messages and/or communications. Marketing creates compelling messages to connect and engage with their target audience over time to help foster customer relationships. The goal is to get the right message to the right prospect and/or customer. (In today's fragmented media marketplace, communications can occur in multiple directions.)

5. Expand your brand. Peter Shankman recommends creating experiences around your brand while Margie Clayman suggests building your brand by convincing your audience of its value.

6. 6. Tell your company's story. According to Ann Handley, marketing is anything you create or share that tells your story.

For Gerry Lantzm, marketing finds the right story to engage consumers in authentic conversations.

7. Have conversations and engage to build lasting relationships. This point goes to the heart of social media. For Trey Pennington, marketing is an on-going process of engagement. Sally Falkow stated it well, "If you build a better mousetrap, people will beat a path to your door" doesn't hold true without marketing. You might indeed have a better mousetrap, but if people don't know you have it, and they don't know where your door is, there will be no path beating and no conversation going on. Rebecca Lieb refers to marketing as a feedback loop that helps the company to inform and shape its business going forward. In Chris Garret's words, marketing is the process of building relationships with prospects and customers. Marketing helps firms connect with real people and create a desire to share.

8. Make customers fall in love with your products and companies. Delight your customers. In Saul Colt's words, create irresistible experiences. Marketing is when your target consumer feels so strongly about your product, brand or company that they integrate it into their daily routines and lifestyles, in Jeanniey Mullen's view.

9. Develop customer trust. This is especially important for marketers who aim to build a community and was mentioned most frequently by marketers heavily involved in social media marketing. (Unfortunately, from the customer's perspective, the trust is gone.) Max Kalehoff recommended that marketing should embrace the highest ethical standards, respect the environment, and strive to make the world a better place.

Jim Siegel suggests earning trust with every contact and transaction.

10. Help sell stuff. While marketing doesn't actually sell, as Jason Falls said, marketing helps people buy your product and/ or service. Marketing is business' play-maker according to Sam Fiorella. In Mary Ellen Bianco's words, marketing prepares an audience to receive a direct sales pitch. For Jeffrey Harmon, marketing is about educating prospects about good products to create a desire. As Steve Dawson said, marketing is products that don't come back.

11.   Everything a company does. For several, marketing was the sum of a variety of functions: branding, naming, pricing, research, branding, PR, advertising, direct response, promotions, loyalty, demand generation and the bridge between paid and earned media. Marketing is an extended process involved in creating strategies and tactics to achieve specific company goals to attract and connect prospects and customers with your products.

12. Drive profits. Marketing should deliver measurable results and increase company value. Interestingly, marketing definitions focused on profits, the money that remains from sales after covering the costs to build and distribute the product and other on-going expenses.

http://www.forbes.com/sites/gregsatell/2013/10/21/what-can-we-expect-from-the-next-decade-of-marketing/

http://heidicohen.com/marketing-elements/

3

Basic Principles

Seven Principles of Marketing

Greg

If it weren't for lawyers, marketers would probably be the most reviled professional class. Rodney Dangerfield has nothing on us.

Lately, the criticism has gotten unusually shrill. One prominent ad agency executive recently said thatmarketing is dead. Somebody else wrote the same inHarvard Business Review. A prominent VC says thatmarketing is just for companies with sucky products. It seems like we never get any respect.

I think that part of the problem stems from the fact that other professions have qualifications. Doctors go to medical school, engineers build things, financiers make money and even lawyers need to get admitted to the bar. Meanwhile, any jackass off the street can call himself a marketer. What we need are concrete principles. Here are seven.

1. More than Half the Value of a Typical Business is Intangible

Many financial types want little to do with marketing. They want to see hard assets, dollars and cents. The last thing they want to hear about is any softheaded notions of brand image. They want us to show them the money. Plain and simple.

Unfortunately, many financial types know little about finance. The fact is that, for most companies, intangible value makes up more than half of the total market value. Take a look at the chart below:

| Estimates of Intangible Value | | | | |
Company	Market Cap	Book Value	Intangible Value	Ratio
Apple	593	76	517	87%
Coke	177	32	145	82%
Pepsi	122	20	88	80%
Kimberly Clark	33	5	20	77%
Google	219	58	161	74%
Wal-Mart	250	71	179	72%
Verizon	126	36	90	71%
Viacom	26	9	17	64%
P&G	188	68	120	64%
exxon	407	154	253	62%
Target	35	15	20	56%
AT&T	214	106	108	50%
Chevron	223	121	102	46%
Time Warner	40	30	10	25%
Source: Yahoo Finance; Values in Billions USD				

The chart compares market capitalization (i.e. the value of a company alive) with book value (the value of a company dead). What's left over is intangible value. If a business was merely a balance sheet, nobody would ever pay more for one than its assets minus its liabilities. Even a casual examination quickly reveals that's not how the real world works.

A few things that I want to point out initially. First, intangible value is enormous, making up the majority of the worth of a successful business. Second, the ratio of intangible value does not depend on the industry (I've color coded competitors to make comparisons easier), the size of the company or even the age of the business.

So what does intangible value depend on? As I've argued before, brands are promises and the value of a business is the value of the promises kept.

2. Marketing is not Advertising or even Promotion, but Identifying "Jobs to be Done"

Another interesting fact borne out of the chart above is that intangible value is not a matter of mere promotion. Wal-Mart has a higher intangible ratio than the more promotionally oriented Target, for example. Even in industries that require enormous capital investment, such as telecom and oil, intangible value is huge.

While effective promotion is obviously a very important part of marketing, it is certainly not the only, nor even the primary task. An effective marketing program identifies consumer needs and preferences, helps determine how those needs can best be met and how much people will be willing to pay for them.

In other words, successful marketing is mostly about finding profitable opportunities forvalue exchange. Often, those opportunities are product related, but they don't need to be. For instance Zynga has unlocked value in people's social relationships while American Express Open Forum has profited by giving their consumers valuable content.

In a nutshell, people need jobs done for them. The main task of marketing is to identify which jobs their organization can do most profitably and make sure people know about it.

3. Owned and Earned Media are More Influential

Watching Mad Men, you get the idea that promotion is all about snappy taglines and slick TV commercials. In the past, that was mostly true, but digital media and the data that came with it, has changed a lot of what we thought we knew. Clearly, we now live in apost-promotional paradigm.

We were always aware that word of mouth existed, but had no idea how powerful it was. The new social era shed light on the fact that recommendations from people we know are more influential than anything else. Further, the digital nature of those recommendations means that they can go viral and get picked up by mainstream media as well.

Owned media, such as websites, Facebook pages and storefronts have the additional advantages of allowing for deep product information, customer service and conversion to purchase. Not surprisingly, publishing has become an increasingly important marketing skill.

4. Paid Media is Easier to Activate

The rise of owned and earned media has caused many to believe that there is no reason to pay for media anymore. That's a mistake. While owned and earned media certainly have some advantages, they don't guarantee that you will reach anybody. There's no use having a party if nobody shows up.

TV is still the best way to reach a majority of your consumers in a short period of time. Want to reach 60% or 70% of your target this week? No problem. Banner ads, while much maligned because of low CTR's, offer more sophisticated forms of targeting and can guarantee you the audience you want.

Most of all, advertising messages are effective. While some believe that they are impervious to brand messages, abundant empirical research says otherwise. Highly sophisticated, profit driven enterprises will spend over $400 billion on paid advertising this year, with good reason.

5. Evaluate the Path to Purchase

One of the most important innovations in recent years is the rise of path to purchase models. They have, in fact, become so pervasive that even consulting giant Mckinsey has gotten into the act. The wide array of different approaches can be confusing, but they all rest on three pillars:

Three Pillars of the Brand

While different brands in different categories might want to add more detail in different places, if you perform in these three areas, chances are that you're doing pretty well. Awareness, sales and advocacy should be considered the three core tasks of any brand and marketers need to continually track those indicators of brand health.

While marketing is still very much alive, promotional strategy needs to embrace new realities and new paradigms. Competitive path to purchase analysis plays an increasingly important role in evaluating opportunities and pointing the way toward effective strategies.

6. Seed, Share and Convert

While the concept of paid, owned and earned media has become pervasive, it really isn't all that useful. It merely provides us with a taxonomy, not a basis for action. What really need to do is to seed, share and convert.

Seeding: When social media first appeared, its advocates claimed that it would mean the end of traditional media. That never happened and it doesn't look like it every will. It soon became clear that marketing without paid media simply doesn't work. Nothing can replace the speed, efficiency and consistency of mass media.

Regular readers of this blog know that I've long advocated a big seed strategy along the lines formulated by network theorist Duncan Watts. The fact that most popular brands on Facebook and Twitter invest heavily in traditional media bears this out.

Sharing: Promoting sharing is problematic because we it's not something we can directly control. Social media strategy is still in its infancy and we are still learning how to do it. My experience is that common sense usually goes a long way. Compelling content, along with respect for the consumer and ample sharing opportunities are good, basic policies.

Converting: Turning prospects into paying customers is another thing marketers generally know how to do well (albeit some better than others). Couponing, website optimization and in-store promotions are all areas of considerable expertise. Shopper marketing has also come a long way in the last decade.

However, recently become an area of vigorous innovation, especially at the point of sale. E-commerce and physical retail are converging with screens technology to create a new digital battlefield and new, mobile marketing technologies such as near field communication will revolutionize how we buy products and services.

7. Marketing is not a Science

As I noted in the beginning, one of the great frustrations of marketing is that we don't really do anything on our own. We don't build things like engineers or argue cases in court like lawyers or even create financial returns like Wall Street traders. We are not successful on our own, but enable others to be. Often, our efforts go unrecognized.

That's led some to focus on what we can quantify and optimize. That's a mistake.Marketing is not a science, but a business function. Much like other worthy endeavors, it is best practiced when it is informed by science and adopts some of its methods, but that is not the same thing.

One person who deeply understood this was Steve Jobs. As I've explained before, he hadlittle talent as an engineer, but had a knack for understanding what kind of jobs consumers wanted done (i.e. 1000 songs in your pocket), a flair for promotion and a deep devotion to building a community of like minded people.

Most of all, he understood that creating efficiency is not the same as creating value. Marketing will live on as long as dreams do. Identifying and fulfilling those dreams is the essence of good marketing and good business.

The Marketing Mix and 4 Ps

Understanding How to Position Your Market Offering

How to use the 4Ps

James Manktelow& Amy Carlson

What is marketing?

The definition that many marketers learn as they start out in the industry is:

Putting the right product in the right place, at the right price, at the right time.

It's simple! You just need to create a product that a particular group of people want, put it on sale some place that those same people visit regularly, and price it at a level which matches the value they feel they get out of it; and do all that at a time they want to buy. Then you've got it made!

There's a lot of truth in this idea. However, a lot of hard work needs to go into finding out what customers want, and identifying where they do their shopping. Then you need to figure out how to produce the item at a price that represents value to them, and get it all to come together at the critical time.

But if you get just one element wrong, it can spell disaster. You could be left promoting a car with amazing fuel-economy in a country where fuel is very cheap; or publishing a textbook after the start of the new school year, or selling an item at a price that's too high – or too low – to attract the people you're targeting.

The marketing mix is a good place to start when you are thinking through your plans for a product or service, and it helps you avoid these kinds of mistakes.

Understanding the Tool

The marketing mix and the 4 Ps of marketing are often used as synonyms for each other. In fact, they are not necessarily the same thing.

"Marketing mix" is a general phrase used to describe the different kinds of choices organizations have to make in the whole process of bringing a product or service to market. The 4Ps is one way – probably the best-known way – of defining the marketing mix, and was first expressed in 1960 by E J McCarthy.

The 4Ps are:

• Product (or Service).

• Place.

• Price.

• Promotion.

A good way to understand the 4Ps is by the questions that you need to ask to define your marketing mix. Here are some questions that will help you understand and define each of the four elements:

Product/Service

• What does the customer want from the product/service? What needs does it satisfy?

• What features does it have to meet these needs?

• Are there any features you've missed out?

• Are you including costly features that the customer won't actually use?

• How and where will the customer use it?

• What does it look like? How will customers experience it?

• What size(s), color(s), and so on, should it be?

• What is it to be called?

• How is it branded?

• How is it differentiated versus your competitors?

• What is the most it can cost to provide, and still be sold sufficiently profitably? (See also Price, below).

Place

• Where do buyers look for your product or service?

• If they look in a store, what kind? A specialist boutique or in a supermarket, or both? Or online? Or direct, via a catalogue?

• How can you access the right distribution channels?

• Do you need to use a sales force? Or attend trade fairs? Or make online submissions? Or send samples to catalogue companies?

• What do you competitors do, and how can you learn from that and/or differentiate?

Price

• What is the value of the product or service to the buyer?

• Are there established price points for products or services in this area?

• Is the customer price sensitive? Will a small decrease in price gain you extra market share? Or will a small increase be indiscernible, and so gain you extra profit margin?

• What discounts should be offered to trade customers, or to other specific segments of your market?

• How will your price compare with your competitors?

Promotion

• Where and when can you get across your marketing messages to your target market?

• Will you reach your audience by advertising in the press, or on TV, or radio, or on billboards? By using direct marketing mailshot? Through PR? On the Internet?

• When is the best time to promote? Is there seasonality in the market? Are there any wider environmental issues that suggest or dictate the timing of your market launch, or the timing of subsequent promotions?

• How do your competitors do their promotions? And how does that influence your choice of promotional activity?

The 4Ps model is just one of many marketing mix lists that have been developed over the years. And, whilst the questions we have listed above are key, they are just a subset of the detailed probing that may be required to optimize your marketing mix.

Amongst the other marketing mix models have been developed over the years is Boom and Bitner's 7Ps, sometimes called the extended marketing mix, which include the first 4 Ps, plus people, processes and physical layout decisions.

Another marketing mix approach is Lauterborn's 4Cs, which presents the elements of the marketing mix from the buyer's, rather than the seller's, perspective. It is made up of Customer needs and wants (the equivalent of product), Cost (price), Convenience (place) and Communication (promotion). In this article, we focus on the 4Ps model as it is the most well-recognized, and contains the core elements of a good marketing mix.

Using the 4Ps Marketing Mix Model

The marketing mix model can be used to help you decide how to take a new offer to market. It can also be used to test your existing marketing strategy. Whether you are considering a new or existing offer, follow the steps below help you define and improve your marketing mix.

1. Start by identifying the product or service that you want to analyze.

2. Now go through and answer the 4Ps questions – as defined in detail above.

3. Try asking "why" and "what if" questions too, to challenge your offer. For example, ask why your target audience needs a particular feature. What if you drop your price by 5%? What if you offer more colors? Why sell through wholesalers rather than direct channels? What if you improve PR rather than rely on TV advertising?

Tip:

Check through your answers to make sure they are based on sound knowledge and facts. If there are doubts about your assumptions, identify any market research, or facts and figures that you may need to gather.

4. Once you have a well-defined marketing mix, try "testing" the overall offer from the customer's perspective, by asking customer focused questions:

1. Does it meet their needs? (product)

2. Will they find it where they shop? (place)

3. Will they consider it's priced favorably? (price)

4. And will the marketing communications reach them? (promotion)

5. Keep on asking questions and making changes to your mix until you are satisfied that you have optimized your marketing mix, given the information and facts and figures you have available.

6. Review you marketing mix regularly, as some elements will need to change as the product or service, and its market, grow, mature and adapt in an ever-changing competitive environment.

Key Points

The marketing mix helps you define the marketing elements for successfully positioning your market offer.

One of the best known models is the Four Ps, which helps you define your marketing options in terms of product, place, price and promotion. Use the model when you are planning a new venture, or evaluating an existing offer, to optimize the impact with your target market.

http://www.mindtools.com/pages/article/newSTR_94.htm

Marketing models that have stood the test of time

Dave Chaffey

You may have noticed we're fans of using practical models as tools to support marketing strategy development? We believe a clear, simple model gives us a framework to assess how we're doing things now compared to our competitors and plan growth strategies for the future. They're also great for communicating the purpose and reason behind a strategy your pursuing.

I think most would agree that models are useful "Mind Tools" to structure thinking and communicate a strategy, but there's a problem – too many models and some are academic rather than of practical application in the "real world". So many marketing models have been developed over the years, that it can be overwhelming to know what to use and when... I was talking to Annmarie Hanlon about the power and challenge of using planning models and we decided it would be good to collaborate to create a free guide where we picked and explained the most useful, practical models for students and professionals alike to share.

Since I'm a digital marketer, I have my own views on the relevance of these, indeed in my books I have often included them. In fact thinking of it, most are included in my [amazon-product text="Internet Marketing: Strategy, Implementation and Practice" type="text"]0273746103[/amazon-product].

So before I wrote the guide I thought it would be nice to share the relevant ones here for anyone passing this way who isn't familiar with them. A hopefully more coherent explanation is available in the free guide!

So this is what I think about their value to today's marketer...

1. 7 Ps of The marketing mix

Product, Price, Place, Promotion, People, Process and Physical evidence – these elements of the marketing mix form the core tactical components of a marketing plan.

Using the Internet to vary the marketing mix						
Product	**Promotion**	**Price**	**Place**	**People**	**Process**	**Physical evidence**
• Quality	• Marketing communications	• Positioning	• Trade channels	• Individuals on marketing activities	• Customer focus	• Sales/staff contact
• Image	• Personal promotion	• List	• Sales support	• Individuals on customer contact	• Business-led	• experience of brand
• Branding	• Sales promotion	• Discounts	• Channel number	• Recruitment	• IT-supported	• Product packaging
• Features	• PR	• Credit	• Segmented channels	• Culture/ image	• Design features	• Online experience
• Variants	• Branding	• Payment methods		• Training and skills	• Research and development	
• Mix	• Direct marketing	• Free or value-added elements		• Remuneration		
• Support						
• Customer service						
• Use occasion						
• Availability						
• Warranties						

Figure 5.1 The elements of the marketing mix

I think it's right this is at the start of the list since it's still widely used and I think is a simple way to think through how a company markets its products. A good model to explain marketing strategy to someone who isn't a marketer. But it suffers from a push mentality completely out-of-keeping with modern digital marketing approaches of listening to and engaging customers in participation through social median marketing.

2. USP

Unique Selling Proposition is the concept that brands should make it clear to potential buyers why they are different and better than the competition.

This is a simple concept and an essential message to communicate online since the core brand message often isn't clear. Here are some examples of websites that communicate their online value proposition well. It's not really a model, so although it was included in the CIM centenary vote it's not included in our guide.

3. Boston Consulting Group Matrix

This well known essential MBA model categorises products in a portfolio as Stars, Cash Cows, Dogs and Question Marks, by looking at market growth and market share.

I find this isn't so applicable in the online marketing world for small and medium businesses – it's more of a Big Business corporate strategy model.

4. Brand positioning map

This model allows marketers to visualise a brand's relative position in the market place by plotting consumer perceptions of the brand and competitor brands against the attributes that drive purchase.

This is a great concept for understanding how customers see a brand. We've included an example in the guide. I can't recall many descriptions of this being applied online. I have seen it used as part of user-testing though in comparing different websites?

The creation of an engaging online brand is so important to success in digital marketing, it's a pity there aren't more effective branding models.

5. Customer Lifetime Value models

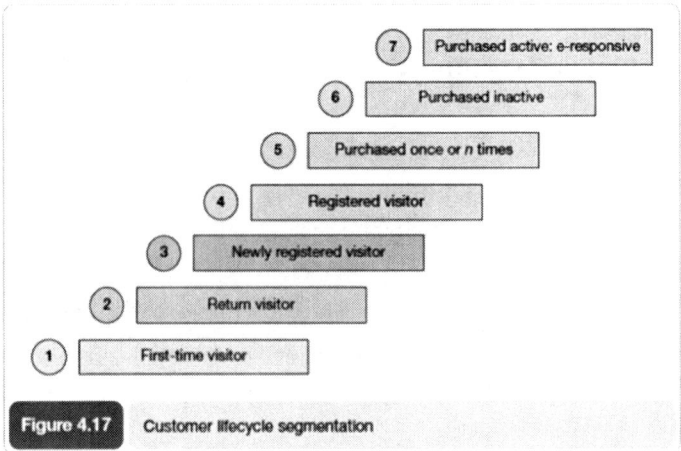

Figure 4.17 Customer lifecycle segmentation

Customer Lifetime Value is the concept used to assess what a customer is worth, based on the present value of future revenue attributed to a customer's relationship with a product.

A different class of models to others, this is more of calculation model – covered in Chapter 6 of my Internet Marketing Book. CLV is mainly important online for transactional sites and certainly investment decisions like allowable cost per acquisition (CPA) must be taken with future customer purchases and attrition rates considered.

6. Growth strategy matrix

Ansoff's matrix identifies alternative growth strategies by looking at present and potential products in current and future markets. The four growth strategies are market penetration, market development, product development and diversification.

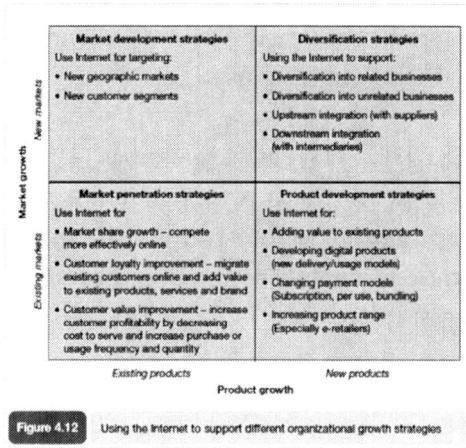

Market development strategies	Diversification strategies
Use Internet for targeting:	Using the Internet to support:
• New geographic markets	• Diversification into related businesses
• New customer segments	• Diversification into unrelated businesses
	• Upstream integration (with suppliers)
	• Downstream integration (with intermediaries)
Market penetration strategies	Product development strategies
Use Internet for	Use Internet for:
• Market share growth – compete more effectively online	• Adding value to existing products
• Customer loyalty improvement – migrate existing customers online and add value to existing products, services and brand	• Developing digital products (new delivery/usage models)
• Customer value improvement – increase customer profitability by decreasing cost to serve and increase purchase or usage frequency and quantity	• Changing payment models (Subscription, per use, bundling)
	• Increasing product range (Especially e-retailers)

Figure 4.12 Using the Internet to support different organizational growth strategies

Ansoff's model dates back to the 1960s, but I still cover it in the books to show how companies should "think out of the box" with their digital strategies by considering new opportunities for market and product development rather than simply market penetration which misses the opportunities of digital marketing for me.

7. Loyalty ladder

This model shows the steps a person takes before becoming loyal to a brand as they move through the stages of prospect, customer, client, supporter and advocate.

Loyalty models are useful as a way of thinking through the opportunities to generate lifetime value.

8. PESTLE

As an extension of the traditional PEST model, this analysis framework is used to assess the impact of macro-environmental factors on a product or brand – political, economical, social, technological, legal and economic.

PESTLE/PEST/DEEPLIST make me groan – to me they're a text book approach which is far removed from improving results. I find students tend to review these in-depth at the expense of creating innovative strategies. The results of the poll seem to suggest others agree.

9. Porter's Five Forces

The five forces are Rivalry, Supplier power, Threat of substitutes, Buyer power and Barriers to entry and are used to analyse the industry context in which the organisation operates.

Yes this one features in my books and I reference a classic 2001 paper by Porter on applying the Five Forces to the Internet. But, I personally think it has limited practical value – yes we know customers have more bargaining power online. So what?! I also think it under-represents the power of intermediaries like comparison sites and publishers in the online world.

10. Product Life Cycle

This model plots the natural path of a product as it moves through the stages of Introduction, Growth, Maturity, Saturation and Decline.

11. Segmentation, Targeting and Positioning

This three stage process involves analysing which distinct customer groups exist and which segment the product best suits before implementing the communications strategy tailored for the chosen target group.

Informed by	Stage of target marketing	Informs
Market research and analysis of customer data	**Segmentation** Identify customer needs and segment market	• Market segment definition • Persona development • Customer experience requirements
Demand analysis	**Target marketing** Evaluate and select target segments	• Select online targeting • Target segments • Online revenue contribution for each segment • Customer lifecycle targeting
Competitor analysis Internal analysis	**Positioning** Identify proposition for each segment	• Core brand proposition • Online value proposition • Online marketing mix • Lifecycle brand development and proposition messaging
Evaluation of resources	**Planning** Deploy resources to achieve plan	• Online marketing mix • Restructuring • Automated online customer contact strategy

Figure 4.15 Stages in target marketing strategy development

As a model which is focused on delivering relevant products, services and communications to the customer and so generating value for an organisation, this is essential for every marketer to understand and apply in practice.

12. PR Smith's SOSTAC® model

This acronym stands for Situation, Objectives, Strategy, Tactics, Actions, Control and is a framework used when creating marketing plans.

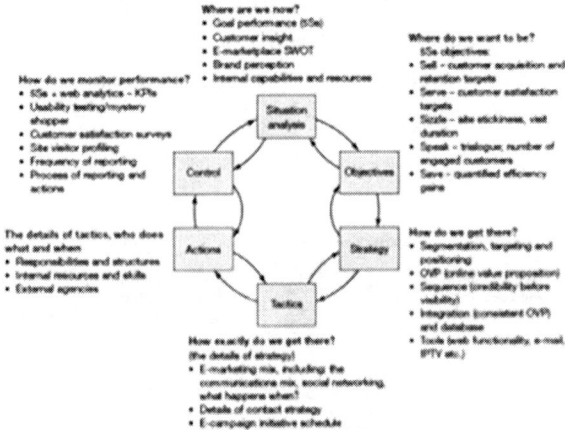

Figure 8.4 SOSTAC™ – a generic framework for e-marketing planning

I'm a big fan of using SOSTAC® as a way of planning and implementing strategies. It features in all my books and I know PR Smith its originator well – he's my co-author on Emarketing Excellence. Check the PDF on his site for more details on how it developed and how to use it.

http://www.smartinsights.com/digital-marketing-strategy/ online-business-revenue-models/marketing-models/

4

MARKETING STRATEGY

How to develop a marketing strategy

Your marketing strategy is, very simply, how you are going to market your products, services or business to customers. It lays out what your objectives are and how you're going to execute them. But that definition is very broad, and a marketing strategy can in fact cover anything from a ten-year vision for marketing your business to how to shift sales on one product over the next three weeks.

As such, the advice here is intended to guide you towards the skeleton of your marketing strategy - you can flesh it out with the help of other guides on Smarta.

What should a marketing strategy achieve?

• Your strategy will depend on where you want your business to go - it forms part of your overall business aims.

• The following are examples of what your overall business aim might be, and marketing strategies that you could use to achieve it:

• Increase sales

• Bring in new customers

• Get existing customers to buy more

• Introduce a new product or service

• Increase market share

• Better establish your brand

• Improve customer loyalty

• Launch an advertising campaign

• Launch a PR campaign

• Encourage word of mouth

• Increase market share

• Retain existing profitable customers

• Make customers feel more valued

• Offer existing customers exclusive offers

• Ensure business stays fresh and new

• Whatever your marketing strategy covers, you should definitely put it down in writing.

• Make everything simple to understand, realistic, and with a clear path of action.

• It will then become part of your longer and more detailed marketing plan - which is the document that deals with a more overarching and long-term view of your business (and so makes up a section of your business plan).

• Be ready to adapt your marketing strategy as and when necessary - there are an infinite number of factors that could require a change. It's flexibility that'll keep you ahead of the competition.

How to develop a marketing strategy, step-by-step

• Research. You need to carry out detailed analyses of these three areas:

• Market analysis: the size of your market, how quickly its growing, your customers and their spending and lifestyle habits.

• Competitor analysis: monitor both direct and indirect competition and how they compare with you on every aspect of sales and marketing (their customers, their brand, price, convenience of location, sales channels, and so on).

• Company analysis: your overall business objectives, how you are going to achieve them, your strengths and weaknesses and those of your products or services.

• Read more about how to carry out this research in our guide on market research.

• Customers. Next you need to identify your target customers, using the information you've gathered from your research and, if needed, more detailed customer research. Then you have to:

• Segment them: split your existing and target customers into groups, according to what they need from your business - which will differ. Some will want cost-effectiveness, some quality, some great customer service, and so on.

• Positioning: how you compare to your competitors for each of your customer segments - are you the fastest, do you have the best customer service, are you the third most popular, and so on.

• Product. Now you need to examine your product or service with the aim of working out how you're going to market it and outdo competitors, according to its:

• USPs: what it can offer that no other product or business can. (Read more in our guide on USPs.)

• Benefits to the customer: From your USPs, draw out what benefits your product or service offers to the customer. These may well vary between your various customer segments. You need to look very closely at what the customer actually sees: while Starbucks sells coffee, the benefit to the customer is a place to relax and have a chat with a friend or a place to sit with a laptop. Your USP may be that you deliver pizza faster than competitors to people in your area, but the benefit to the customer is that they don't have to cook and can receive a ready-made meal quickly. The way you define the benefits will shape your marketing message.

• Communication. How you are now going to communicate the benefits of buying your product or service or using your business to your target customers (again, this may well vary between your various customer segments).

• Marketing mix: the combination of all the marketing tools you are going to use to communicate your benefits to your customers, including and for example: advertising, PR, word of mouth, distribution channels, pricing, promotion, which products you'll sell to them, display in a shop, website, and so on.

• Remembering four P's can be useful when you're putting your marketing mix together: Product, Placing, Pricing, Promotion.

The marketing plan

• Having developed your strategy, you can now write it into a marketing plan.

• The plan goes into the logistical details of executing your strategy, such as budgets, more detailed timescales, who within your company will manage the various points of the strategy, the logistics of various distribution channels and their incumbent costs and so on.

• As such, it is of course a longer and more detailed document.

• Your marketing plan is typically a more live document than your strategy (meaning you will tweak and update it more regularly). As costings, market conditions, economic conditions and other factors change, you'll need to adjust your plan to accommodate them - whereas your strategy could well remain the same.

• For both your strategy and your plan to be useful, you need to closely monitor the results of marketing activity, and be ready to adapt both as necessary.

Jargon buster

Marketing mix: the combination of all the marketing tools you are going to use to communicate your benefits to your customers, including and for example: advertising, PR, word of mouth, distribution channels, pricing, promotion, which products you'll sell to them, display in a shop, website, and so on. In a nutshell: product, placing, pricing and promotion.

Marketing Plan Template: Exactly What To Include

To grow your business, you need a marketing plan. The right marketing plan identifies everything from 1) who your target customers are to 2) how you will reach them, to 3) how you will retain your customers so they repeatedly buy from you.

Done properly, your marketing plan will be the roadmap you follow to get unlimited customers and dramatically improve the success of your organization. To help you succeed, use this proven marketing plan template, and the information below details the 15 key sections you must include in your marketing plan.

Section 1: Executive Summary

Complete your Executive Summary last, and, as the name implies, this section merely summarizes each of the other sections of your marketing plan.

Your Executive Summary will be helpful in giving yourself and other constituents (e.g., employees, advisors, etc.) an overview of your plan.

Section 2: Target Customers

This section describes the customers you are targeting. It defines their demographic profile (e.g., age, gender), psychographic profile (e.g., their interests) and their precise wants and needs as they relate to the products and/or services you offer.

Being able to more clearly identify your target customers will help you both pinpoint your advertising (and get a higher return on investment) and better "speak the language" of prospective customers.

Section 3: Unique Selling Proposition (USP)

Having a strong unique selling proposition (USP) is of critical importance as it distinguishes your company from competitors.

The hallmark of several great companies is their USP. For example, FedEx's USP of "When it absolutely, positively has to be there overnight" is well-known and resonates strongly with customers who desire reliability and quick delivery.

Section 4: Pricing & Positioning Strategy

Your pricing and positioning strategy must be aligned. For example, if you want your company to be known as the premier brand in your industry, having too low a price might dissuade customers from purchasing.

In this section of your marketing plan, detail the positioning you desire and how your pricing will support it.

Section 5: Distribution Plan

Your distribution plan details how customers will buy from you. For example, will customers purchase directly from you on your website? Will they buy from distributors or other retailers? And so on.

Think through different ways in which you might be able to reach customers and document them in this section of your marketing plan.

Section 6: Your Offers

Offers are special deals you put together to secure more new customers and drive past customers back to you.

Offers may include free trials, money-back guarantees, packages (e.g., combining different products and/or services) and discount offers. While your business doesn't necessarily require offers, using them will generally cause your customer base to grow more rapidly.

Section 7: Marketing Materials

Your marketing materials are the collateral you use to promote your business to current and prospective customers. Among others, they include your website, print brochures, business cards, and catalogs.

Identify which marketing materials you have completed and which you need created or re-done in this section of your plan.

Section 8: Promotions Strategy

The promotions section is one of the most important sections of your marketing plan and details how you will reach new customers.

There are numerous promotional tactics, such as television ads, trade show marketing, press releases, online advertising, and event marketing.

In this section of your marketing plan, consider each of these alternatives and decide which ones will most effectively allow you to reach your target customers.

Section 9: Online Marketing Strategy

Like it or not, most customers go online these days to find and/ or review new products and/or services to purchase. As such, having the right online marketing strategy can help you secure new customers and gain competitive advantage.

The four key components to your online marketing strategy are as follows:

1. Keyword Strategy: identify what keywords you would like to optimize your website for.

2. Search Engine Optimization Strategy: document updates you will make to your website so it shows up more prominently for your top keywords.

3. Paid Online Advertising Strategy: write down the online advertising programs will you use to reach target customers.

4. Social Media Strategy: document how you will use social media websites to attract customers.

Section 10: Conversion Strategy

Conversion strategies refer to the techniques you employ to turn prospective customers into paying customers.

For example, improving your sales scripts can boost conversions. Likewise increasing your social proof (e.g., showing testimonials of past clients who were satisfied with your company) will nearly always boost conversions and sales.

In this section of your plan, document which conversion-boosting strategies you will use.

Section 11: Joint Ventures & Partnerships

Joint ventures and partnerships are agreements you forge with other organizations to help reach new customers or better monetize existing customers. For example, if you sold replacement guitar strings, it could be quite lucrative to partner with a guitar manufacturer who had a list of thousands of customers to whom it sold guitars (and who probably need replacement strings in the future).

Think about what customers buy before, during and/or after they buy from your company. Many of the companies who sell these products and/or services could be good partners. Document such companies in this section of your marketing plan and then reach out to try to secure them.

Section 12: Referral Strategy

A strong customer referral program could revolutionize your success. For example, if every one of your customers referred one new customer, your customer base would constantly grow.

However, rarely will you get such growth unless you have a formalized referral strategy. For example, you need to determine when you will ask customers for referrals, what if anything you will give them as a reward, etc. Think through the best referral strategy for your organization and document it.

Section 13: Strategy for Increasing Transaction Prices

While your primary goal when conversing with prospective customers is often to secure the sale, it is also important to pay attention to the transaction price.

The transaction price, or amount customers pay when they buy from you, can dictate your success. For example, if your average customer transaction is $100 but your competitor's average customer transaction is $150, they will generate more revenues, and probably profits, per customer. As a result, they will be able to outspend you on advertising, and continue to gain market share at your expense.

In this section of your plan, think about ways to increase your transaction prices such as by increasing prices, creating product or service bundles/packages, and so on.

Section 14: Retention Strategy

Too many organizations spend too much time and energy trying to secure new customers versus investing in getting existing customers to buy more often.

By using retention strategies such as a monthly newsletter or customer loyalty program, you can increase revenues and profits by getting customers to purchase from you more frequently over time.

Identify and document ways you can better retain customers here.

Section 15: Financial Projections

The final part of your marketing plan is to create financial projections. In your projections, include all the information documented in your marketing plan.

For example, include the promotional expenses you expect to incur and what your expected results will be in terms of new customers, sales and profits. Likewise include your expected results from your new retention strategy. And so on.

While your financial projections will never be 100% accurate, use them to identify which promotional expenses and other strategies should give you the highest return on investment. Also, by completing your financial projections, you will set goals (e.g., your goals for your referral program) for which your company should strive.

Completing each of the 15 sections of your marketing plan is real work. But, once your marketing plan is complete, it will be worth it, as your sales and profits should soar.

5

Marketing Techniques and Methods

Andrew Beattie

Seven Popular Marketing Techniques For Small Businesses

Before your business starts marketing a product, it helps to create an ideal customer who you want to reach with your promotional materials. Once you have your ideal customer, you have a plethora of techniques to pick from. Most of these are low cost/no cost methods (sometimes called guerrilla marketing) and you may use different ones at different stages of your business cycle, or you may utilize them all at once from your business' inception. We'll look at seven of these techniques in more detail. (Do you have what it takes to work in this fast-paced field? This article will help you determine if marketing is for you. Refer to A Career Guide For Marketing Majors.)

Hooray for Free Advertising

When you build a business, the first thing you want to secure is a customer base. With a decent printer, an answering machine and an average computer, you can put together a fairly extensive advertising campaign without having to pay for space.

1. Flyers

This is the carpet-bombing method of cheap advertising. You find an area that you would like to do business in and you distribute flyers to all the mailboxes within reach. Your flyer should be brief and to the point, highlighting the services you offer and providing contact information. Offering a free appraisal, coupon or discount never hurts.

2. Posters

Most supermarkets, public spaces and malls offer free bulletin board space for announcements and advertisements. This is a hit or miss method, but you should try to make your poster reasonably visible and have removable tabs that the customers can present for a discount. Make each location a different color so that you can get an idea from the tabs where the most leads are being generated. If there is one area that is producing the majority of your leads, you can better target your campaign (flyers, ads in papers catering to those areas, cold calling, etc.)

3. Value Additions

This is one of the most powerful selling points for any product or service. On the surface, value additions are very similar to coupons and free appraisals, but they are aimed at increasing customer satisfaction and widening the gap between you and competition.

Common value additions include guarantees, discounts for repeat customers, point cards and referrals rewards. Often the deciding factor for a person picking between one of two similar shops is whether he or she has a point card or preferred customer card. You don't have to promise the moon to add value; often you just have to state something that the customer may not realize about your product or service. When you are making your advertising materials, the value additions should be highlighted.

4. Referral Networks

Referral networks are invaluable to a business. This does not only mean customer referrals, which are encouraged though discounts or other rewards per referral. This includes business-to-business referrals. If you have ever found yourself saying, "we don't do/sell that here, but X down the street does," you should make certain that you are getting a referral in return.

When dealing with white-collar professions, this network is even stronger. A lawyer refers people to an accountant, an accountant refers people a broker, a financial planner refers people to a real estate agent - in each of these situations, the person stakes his or her professional reputation on the referral. Regardless of your business, make sure you create a referral network that has the same outlook and commitment to quality that you do.

As a final note on referral networks, remember that your competition is not always your enemy. If you are too busy to take a job, throw it their way, most times you will find the favor returned. Besides, it can be bad for your reputation if a customer has to wait too long. (Are your shoulder's wide enough to carry a company's reputation? See The Marketing Director's Pitch.)

5. Follow-Up

Advertising can help you get a job, but what you do after a job can often be a much stronger marketing tool. Follow-up questionnaires are one of the best sources of feedback for how your ad campaign is going. Why did the customer choose your business? Where did he or she hear about it? Which other companies had he or she considered? What was the customer most satisfied with? What was least satisfying? Also, if your job involves going to the customer, make sure to slip a flyer into the nearby mailboxes, as people of similar needs and interests tend to live in the same area.

6. Cold Calling

Unpleasant? Yes. Important? Yes. Cold calling, whether it is over the phone or door to door, is a baptism of fire for many small businesses. Cold calling forces you to sell yourself as well as your business. If people can't buy you, the person talking to them, then they won't buy anything from you. Over the phone you don't have the benefit of a smile or face-to-face conversation – a phone is a license for people to be as caustic and abrupt as possible (we are all guilty of this at one time or another). However, cold calling does makes you think on your feet and encourages creativity and adaptability when facing potential customers.

7. The Internet

It is dishonest to pretend that the Internet is a cohesive whole for marketing – like a community hall you can put up a poster in or a section of the highway were you can buy billboard space. However, it is difficult to overstate the importance the Internet has on marketing. The previous methods of marketing have not changed in the last 50 years. The Internet has been born and evolved rapidly during that same time frame.

It is nearly unthinkable that a company, even a local café will not have at least a website with the vital details such as location and hours. Not having a site means not having a point of access for the growing number of people who Google first when they want to make a buying decision. Add to this a social media presence (Facebook page, Twitter account) and the need for good SEO, and it can appear overwhelming. However, the technology has evolved to the point where Wordpress – just one example of a free HTML editor – can meet all these needs.

Bottom Line

More than likely, you will find that the conversion rate on marketing is very low. Even the most successful campaigns measure leads – and converted sales from those leads - in the 10-20% range. This helps to shatter any illusions about instant success, but it is also an opportunity for improvement. Do you want a company to buy your product? Give them a presentation showing how it will benefit them. Do you want someone to use your service? Give them an estimate or a sample of what you will do for them. Be confident, creative and unapologetic – people will eventually respond. (Understanding how to manage business credit is the key to obtaining small business loans. Check out The Small Business Jobs Act: Make It Work For You.)

http://www.investopedia.com/articles/financial-theory/11/small-business-marketing-techniques.asp

Marketing techniques

A marketing strategy is an overall marketing plan designed to meet the needs and requirements of customers. The plan should be based on clear objectives. A number of techniques will then be employed to make sure that the marketing plan is effectively delivered. Marketing techniques are the tools used by the marketing department. The marketing department will set out to identify the most appropriate techniques to employ in order to make profits. These marketing techniques include public relations, trade and consumer promotions, point-of-sale materials, editorial, publicity and sales literature.

Marketing techniques are employed at three stages of marketing:

Stage 1 Prior to marketing activity	Stage 2 During marketing activity	Stage 3 After marketing activity
Market research	Developing the marketing mix	Evaluation of marketing effectiveness

Market research enables the organisation to identify the most appropriate marketing mix. The mix should consist of:

• the right product

• sold at the right price

• in the right place

• using the most suitable promotional techniques.

To create the right marketing mix, marketers have to ensure the following:

• The product has to have the right features - for example, it must look good and work well.

• The price must be right. Consumers will need to buy in large numbers to produce a healthy profit.

• The goods must be in 'the right place at the right time'. Making sure that the goods arrive when and where they are wanted is an important operation.

• The target group needs to be aware of the existence and availability of the product through promotion. Successful promotion helps a firm to spread costs over a larger output.

Finally techniques need to be applied to monitor the success of marketing activity. For example when carrying out advertising it is helpful to track consumer awareness of the adverts and their messages. Evaluation can also take the place of other aspects of the marketing mix e.g. which distribution channels were most effective? Was the chosen price the right one? etc.

Business behaviour: marketing

Today businesses have an increasing market focus. If organisations are to serve the needs of their customers they need to be structured in such a way as to identify and meet customer requirements.

Businesses therefore need to behave in such a way that they recognise the needs of the customer.

A company prospers best when everyone in it believes that success depends on the excellence of his or her contribution.

Short-term decisions made many times a day by individuals determine the quality of that day's work.

The governing principle should be that everybody has a customer - either outside the company (the traditional 'customer') or inside the company (the internal customer). Both kinds of customer expect to be supplied with the product or service they need, on time and as specified.

The principle holds good for everyone in the company, whatever their level of skill and experience, whether their 'product' is answering a telephone in a helpful way or masterminding a major new project. It works to everyone's benefit. It gives the individual genuine responsibility and scope for initiative and it virtually guarantees that the company's performance will be improved.

However, individual behaviours will only match the organisation objective of being customer focused if the right sorts of structures are created. Hence the importance of developing structures such as team working and empowering employees to make decisions rather than be told what to do.

Modern companies like Travis Perkins (builders merchants), and Argos (catalogue retailer) have recognised the importance of team working in motivating employees and in providing close links to the consumer. By encouraging staff to listen to consumers these organisations are best placed to provide the products and the services that ensure ongoing business success.

Empowerment is the process of giving increased power and responsibility to employees at all levels within an organisation. It involves placing more trust in them.

Decentralisation is the process of handing down power from the corporate centre (e.g. Head Office) to the various parts of the organisation.

Advertising, promotion, packaging and branding

Advertising, promotion, packaging and branding are important marketing tools which are used to make products and services more desirable and hence increase sales and profits.

Any form of publicity is advertising. There are two main forms of advertising although in practice the two are inter-related.

The informational aspect of advertising involves providing information about products, services, or about important issues. For example, the government provides information about the dangers of cigarette smoking, which is an example of informative advertising.

Persuasive advertising goes further and uses a persuasive message, for example by:

• showing a famous personality (e.g. Gary Lineker) using the product

• comparing the advantages of one product with another

- using sex appeal.

There are a number of processes involved in producing effective advertising, including:

- identifying the most appropriate market segments to target the advertising

- choosing the best possible media, e.g. television, radio, posters etc

- projecting the right message in the adverts

- getting the timing of the advertisements right

- tracking the effectiveness of the advertising, e.g. checking to see how many people can recall the advert and its message.

Advertising is just one way of promoting a product. Promotion is the business of communicating with customers. There are a number of ways of promoting products and services, including:

- in-store promotion e.g. giving away free samples in a supermarket

- publicity in the media, competitions, and sponsorship

- PR - public relations activities - i.e. presenting the public image of a company to a wide audience

- presenting products in attractive packaging

• creating an attractive brand for a product.

Sponsorship

Packaging typically refers to the material in which a product is packed - or more specifically, the surface design on the material. However, a wider definition includes all the various aspects of presenting a product - e.g. the shape size and appearance of the packaging, colour and design, the convenience of using the packaging etc.

A brand is a product with a unique, consistent and well recognised character. The branding of the product therefore involves projecting and developing this character. The uniqueness can come either from an actual product or from its image - usually created by its manufacturer through advertising and packaging. The consistency comes mainly from the consistency of its quality and performance, but it also reflects the consistency of the advertising and packaging. A brand is well-recognised because it has been around for a long time. It takes years to develop a brand.

Shell has spent over a hundred years developing its brand image through the well known Shell pecten. Audi is associated with its easily recognised four rings logo. McDonald's is associated with its twin arches. Sponsorship is an important way of promoting the name of an organisation. Many sports and arts organisations rely on support from sponsors. For example Vodafone is a major sponsor of Manchester United Football Club, and Bic sponsored Martin Johnson the England World Cup rugby captain.

In return for sponsorship of a sports club or arts event the name of the sponsor will be mentioned prominently on advertising hordings, publicity materials, programmes and other literature associated with the club or event.

The term 'above-the-line' advertising and promotion refers to media such as TV, radio and press, for which commission is paid to an advertising agency. 'Below-the-line' comprises all media and promotional techniques for which fees are paid in preference to commissions - these might include exhibitions, sales literature and direct mail.

http://businesscasestudies.co.uk/business-theory/marketing/ marketing-techniques.html#axzz31nn3NinO

http://businesscasestudies.co.uk/business-theory/marketing/ marketing-techniques.html#ixzz31o8rVjdt

6

BUDGETTING & FINANCIAL PLANNING / ANALYSIS

Introduction to accounting for marketers

Whilst it is not necessary to be a qualified accountant or bookkeeper, a basic understanding of what is involved in financial analysis is essential for anyone in marketing. It is too enticing, and often too easy, to use "blue skies" thinking in planning marketing activities. It is even easier to spend money without fully realising the return one is getting for it. It is behoven, therefore, on marketers, to be more disciplined and analytical in the way they go about planning, executing and evaluating marketing plans and strategy. One way of introducing more discipline into the process is by having a basic understanding of the financial implications of decision making, and how financial measures can be used to monitor and control marketing operations. The purpose of this text is to provide exactly that, and the first chapter deals basically with an introduction to the activities involved in financial analysis.

This chapter is intended to provide:

• An understanding of financial analysis in marketing

• An explanation of the various activities associated with marketing financial analysis

• A brief introduction to the various financial analysis methods.

Structure of the chapter

The chapter introduces the way in which financial analysis can be used in marketing, and gives a brief overview of the areas in marketing where a knowledge of finance can be very useful, particularly in helping marketers gauge how well strategy is working, in evaluating marketing research alternatives, developing future plans and in marketing control.

The marketing financial analysis circle

Financial analysis can be used to serve many purposes in an organisation but in the area of marketing it has four main functions:

a) to gauge how well marketing strategy is working (situation analysis)

b) to evaluate marketing decision alternatives

c) to develop plans for the future

d) to control activities on a short term or-day to-day basis.

In effect these four functions comprise what can be called the "Marketing Financial Analysis Circle" (see figure 1.1)

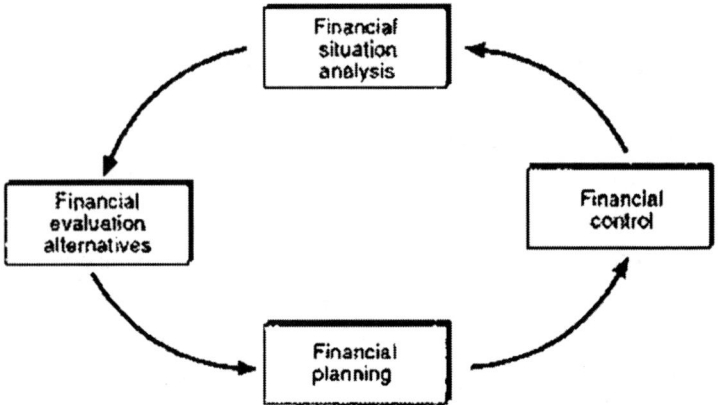

Figure 1.1 The marketing-financial analysis circle

Activities associated with marketing financial analysis functions

For each of the four functional areas where financial analysis is useful in marketing, there are a number of associated activities viz:

a) Financial situation analysis (how well marketing strategy is working)

This involves the study of:

• the study of trends

• comparative analysis

• assessment of present financial strengths and limitations for the whole business, brand or component of the business, e.g. transportation.

b) Financial evaluation of alternatives

This involves the study of a number of factors like the market place, competitors etc., and is used for decisions whether to:

• introduce new products/delete mature products

• expand the sales force or do more advertising

• delete a market operation e.g. close a Dairy Board depot or increase the sales fleet

• move into a new market or markets

• build a new grain depot or silo.

c) Financial planning (projections concerning activities which marketing management has decided to undertake)

Financial planning is used for a number of activities like:

- the introduction of a new range of products

- the forecasting of sales and costs

- market liberalisation.

d) Financial control (actual compared to planned results)

This activity is mainly centered around keeping plans on course.

Methods involved in marketing financial analysis

There are a variety of methods used in each of the four functional areas. Some of these include the following:

a) Financial situation analysis

- Ratio analysis

- Profit and contribution analysis

- Sales and cost analysis.

b) Financial evaluation of alternatives

- Sales and costs analysis

- Break even analysis

• Profit contribution, cash flow analysis, profit projections

• Return on investment

• Return on capital employed

• Sustainable growth rates.

c) Financial planning

• Sales and costs forecasts

• Budgets

• Proforma income statements.

d) Financial control

• Sales and costs forecasts

• Actual results compared to budgets (analysis of variance)

• Profit performance.

What is analysed in marketing financial analysis

Two factors influence the choice of unit of analysis:

a) the purpose of the analysis

b) the cost of the information needed to perform the analysis.

Several possible units can be used in marketing financial analysis and cost or sales data can be used. These units are listed in table 1.1. which is by no means exhaustive. Units can be chosen which suit the particular situation or organisation.

Table 1.1 - Alternative units in financial analysis

Market	Product/service	Organisation
Total Market	Industry	Company
Market segment (s)	Product mix	Segment/Division/Unit
Geographical areas	Product line	Marketing department
- demographics	Specific product	Sales unit
- product	- brand	Regions
- characteristics	- model	District/Branch
	- size	Office/Store
	- shape	Sales person

Basic financial analysis methods

These will be expanded on in later chapters, so this section serves as an introduction only.

Use of ratios

Ratios can be used to judge the organisation's "liquidity", i.e. can it pay its bills, its "leverage", i.e. how is it financed and its "activities", i.e. the productivity and efficiency of the organisation. Taking liquidity analysis only, this has a bearing on new product planning, marketing budgets and the marketing decisions. Liquidity analysis is drawn from the balance sheet, e.g.:

	$		$
Cash	250	Current	120
Accounts receivable	300	Short term debt	100
Stock	200	Long term debt	1,500
Total current assets	750	Total liabilities	1,720
Property and equipment	2,000	Net worth	1,430
Other assets	400		
Total assets	3,150	Total liabilities and net worth	3,150

Current and quick ratios

These are used to judge a firm's short term capacity to meet its financial responsibilities.

(i) Current ratio

  (should be greater than 1)

750/220=3.41

ii) Quick ratio

  (minus stock)

550/220=2.50

Debt ratios

These are used to measure long term liquidity

  (Current Liability + Short Term Debt + Long Term debt) should be >1

1,720/1,430=1.21

(Long Term Debt + Net Worth)

1,500/2,930=0.51

This ratio shows the extent of leverage (debt) in total capitalisation.

Profit analysis

Breakeven analysis is a method used to estimate the number of units (volume) or sales value required to make neither profit or losses. In other words, it is the point where costs of production and sales volume are equal.

Sales and cost information are used to calculate the breakeven point. Without getting into the argument as to what constitutes fixed or variable costs, fixed costs are defined as those which do not vary with output e.g. rent, rates, whereas variable costs do vary with increased or decreased output, e.g. labour, materials. Breakeven assumes fixed costs are constant, variable costs vary at a constant rate and there is only one selling price. However, with a higher or lower price, the breakeven point will be lower or higher respectively. Breakeven is calculated by the formula:

By rearranging the formula breakeven costs or sales can be calculated. Note that profit level intentions should be added to the fixed costs as this is a "charge" to the company. Also, if one wishes to recover all new investment (value) immediately it should be added to fixed cost.

Breakeven can be calculated by the formula or by graphical methods. Figure 1.2 shows an example of both.

Figure 1.2 Formula and graphical solution for breakeven analysis

i) Formula

Price/Unit = $ 1.846

Variable cost/Unit = $ 0.767

Fixed costs = $70.000

= 65, 000 units (volume)

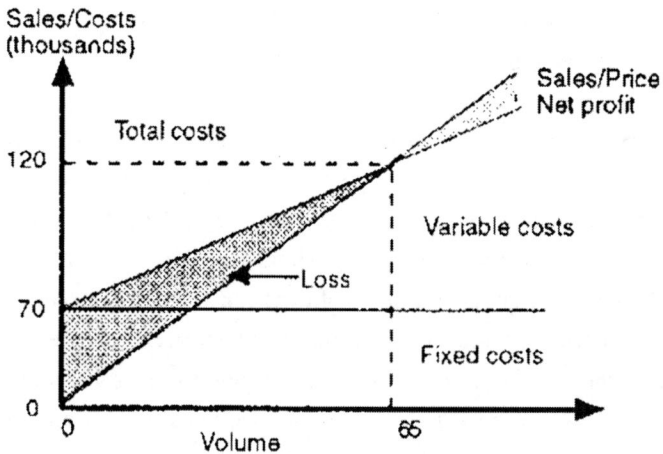

Figure 1.2 Graphical solution

Contribution analysis: When performance of products, market segments and other marketing units is being analysed, an examination of the profit contribution generated by a unit is often very useful to management.

CONTRIBUTION = SALES (REVENUE) - VARIABLE COSTS

So, contribution represents the amount of money available to cover fixed costs and the excess available is net income.

For example, suppose a product is generating a positive contribution margin. If the product is dropped, the remaining products would have to cover fixed costs that are not directly traceable to it.

In the example below if X was eliminated, $50, 000 of product net income would be lost. If the product was retained the $50, 000 could be used to contribute to other fixed costs and/or net income (see figure 1.3.).

Gross and net profit margins: Contribution margin is useful for examining the financial performance of products, market segments and other marketing, planning and control units. However, marketing executives should be familiar with the calculation of gross and net profit margins, which is useful to gauge company and business unit financial performance and to budget for future operations. The profit and loss statement is useful for reporting performance to stockholders and to compute taxes. Figure 1.4 gives an example

Figure 1.3 Illustrative contribution margin for product X (000's)

$

SALES   500

LESS: Variable manufacturing costs   200

        Other variable costs traceable to product X   100

EQUALS: Contribution margin   200

LESS: Fixed cost traceable to product X   150

EQUALS: Product's net income   50

Note: Chapter 5 provides further explanations of a) and b).

Figure 1.4 Illustrative profit and loss statement

$

SALES REVENUE   1,200,000

LESS   Cost of goods sold   800,000

EQUALS: Gross profit margin   400,000

LESS: Selling and admin. expenses   200,000

EQUALS: Net profit before tax   200,000

LESS: Tax   80,000

EQUALS: Net profit   120,000

Consider the following sample data taken from Rowe, Mason, Dickel and Westcott (1987)

$

Cost of goods sold   12,000

Operating expenses   3,600

Sales   16,500

Stocks   3,200

Accounts receivable   3,750

Cash   400

Prepaid expenses   50

Fixed assets   1,200

Financial analysis models

Many models, often computerised, have been developed to aid marketers see the effects on the "bottom line" of a change in an organisation. One such programme is the Dupont Analysis The model allows executives to input data into blank boxes and by manipulating any figure find the resulting outcome. One of the advantages of computer based models is that one can work "backward" or "forward" through the model, setting desired levels of cost or outcomes and calculating the results.

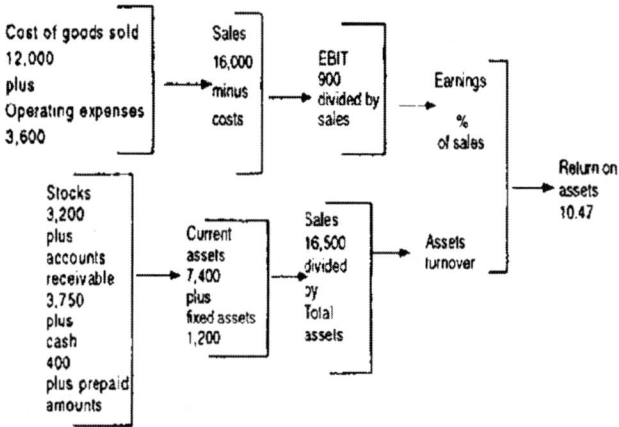

Figure 1.5 Sample printout of the Dupont analysis

Other performance measures

Various other performance measures can be used; these include productivity measures, which, say, for a supermarket would be:

Other measures include inventory turnover:

Budgeting and forecasting

These two activities are essential to marketing planning and are often done via pro forma statements.

a) Marketing budgets

Field sales expense, advertising expense, product development expense, market research expense, distribution expense (trade and administration), promotion expense (trade, consumer).

b) Pro forma financial statement

Annual profit and loss statement, next year pro forma/quarter, current year budget/quarter, last year actual/quarter, annual revision of 5 year pro forma profit and loss statement (expense detail for broad categories).

N.B. In all figures watch for inflation and information gaps (use approximation).

Spreadsheets

Spreadsheets are often used in budgeting and forecasting exercises. Spreadsheets use the memory of a computer as if it were a large piece of paper divided up into a matrix of cells. Into these cells may be entered numbers, text and formulae. The power of these systems is that the data held in any one cell can be made dependent on that held in other cells and changing a value in one cell can set (if wanted) a chain reaction of changes through other related cells. This means that a model can be built in which the effect of changing key parameters may be observed. A term often used to describe spreadsheets is "what if software". It can be used, for example, to evaluate the effect of changing the sales commission rate. Simply entering a new value in the commission rate cell will lead to the automatic re-calculation of all dependent cells. Figure 1.6 shows an example of a spreadsheet used in accounting.

Figure 1.6 A sample spreadsheet

A	B	C	D	E	F
1 Quarterly sales figures					
2					
3 Salesman	1st Qtr	2nd Qtr	3rd Qtr	4th Qtr	Total
4					
5 Alan Adams	5600.00	8750.00	10500.00	8500.00	33350.00
6 Brian Brown	5250.00	7500.00	9500.00	8625.00	30875.00
7 Chris Cooke	5625.00	8250.00	8200.00	9500.00	31575.00
8 Don Davis	4585.00	6500.00	6500.00	7200.00	25810.00
9					

10 Total   21060.00

11

12 Commission   1.5%

13

14 Salesman	1st Qtr	2nd Qtr	3rd Qtr	4th Qtr	Total
15					
16 Alan Adams	84.00	131.25	157.50	127.50	5000.25
17 Brian Brown		78.75	112.50	142.50	129.38	463.13
18 Chris Cooke	84.38	123.75	123.00	142.50	473.63
19 Don Davis	68.78	97.50	112.88	108.00	387.15

Note: The formatting of the 'cells' to display numerical fields to two decimal places/values for commission in the lower half are found by multiplying the sales figures by 1.5%; totals are stored as the SUM (column or row); the borders showing column letters and row numbers may be omitted.

Spreadsheets are powerful personal decision support tools. In addition, programming facilities such as IF...THEN...ELSE greatly extend the control that may be built into the model.

http://www.fao.org/docrep/w4343e/w4343e02.htm

7

Branding

The Basics of Branding

Learn what this critical business term means and what you can do to establish one for your company.

Branding is one of the most important aspects of any business, large or small, retail or B2B. An effective brand strategy gives you a major edge in increasingly competitive markets. But what exactly does "branding" mean? How does it affect a small business like yours?

Simply put, your brand is your promise to your customer. It tells them what they can expect from your products and services, and it differentiates your offering from your competitors'. Your brand is derived from who you are, who you want to be and who people perceive you to be.

Are you the innovative maverick in your industry? Or the experienced, reliable one? Is your product the high-cost, high-quality option, or the low-cost, high-value option? You can't be both, and you can't be all things to all people. Who you are should be based to some extent on who your target customers want and need you to be.

The foundation of your brand is your logo. Your website, packaging and promotional materials--all of which should integrate your logo--communicate your brand.

Brand Strategy & Equity

Your brand strategy is how, what, where, when and to whom you plan on communicating and delivering on your brand messages. Where you advertise is part of your brand strategy. Your distribution channels are also part of your brand strategy. And what you communicate visually and verbally are part of your brand strategy, too.

Consistent, strategic branding leads to a strong brand equity, which means the added value brought to your company's products or services that allows you to charge more for your brand than what identical, unbranded products command. The most obvious example of this is Coke vs. a generic soda. Because Coca-Cola has built a powerful brand equity, it can charge more for its product--and customers will pay that higher price.

The added value intrinsic to brand equity frequently comes in the form of perceived quality or emotional attachment. For example, Nike associates its products with star athletes, hoping customers will transfer their emotional attachment from the athlete to the product. For Nike, it's not just the shoe's features that sell the shoe.

Defining Your Brand

Defining your brand is like a journey of business self-discovery. It can be difficult, time-consuming and uncomfortable. It requires, at the very least, that you answer the questions below:

• What is your company's mission?

• What are the benefits and features of your products or services?

• What do your customers and prospects already think of your company?

• What qualities do you want them to associate with your company?

Do your research. Learn the needs, habits and desires of your current and prospective customers. And don't rely on what you think they think. Know what they think.

Because defining your brand and developing a brand strategy can be complex, consider leveraging the expertise of a nonprofit small-business advisory group or a Small Business Development Center .

Once you've defined your brand, how do you get the word out? Here are a few simple, time-tested tips:

• Get a great logo. Place it everywhere.

• Write down your brand messaging. What are the key messages you want to communicate about your brand? Every employee should be aware of your brand attributes.

• Integrate your brand. Branding extends to every aspect of your business--how you answer your phones, what you or your salespeople wear on sales calls, your e-mail signature, everything.

• Create a "voice" for your company that reflects your brand. This voice should be applied to all written communication and incorporated in the visual imagery of all materials, online and off. Is your brand friendly? Be conversational. Is it ritzy? Be more formal. You get the gist.

• Develop a tagline. Write a memorable, meaningful and concise statement that captures the essence of your brand.

• Design templates and create brand standards for your marketing materials. Use the same color scheme, logo placement, look and feel throughout. You don't need to be fancy, just consistent.

• Be true to your brand. Customers won't return to you--or refer you to someone else--if you don't deliver on your brand promise.

• Be consistent. I placed this point last only because it involves all of the above and is the most important tip I can give you. If you can't do this, your attempts at establishing a brand will fail.

John Williams

John Williams is the founder and president of LogoYes.com, the world's first do-it-yourself logo design website. During John's 25 years in advertising, he's created brand standards for Fortune 100 companies like Mitsubishi and won numerous awards for his design work.

http://www.entrepreneur.com/article/77408

Components that comprise a Comprehensive Brand Strategy

Lauren Sorenson

Your brand's strategy should be based on company goals. And just like James Bond wouldn't have gotten too far without a plan, your business will eventually hit a wall without a cohesive brand strategy. Sure, maybe you can finagle a big sale or trick a Russian spy or two, but one day you'll wake up and have no idea how your company got from A-to-Q -- it's supposed to go from A-to-B, remember? And skipping steps is not how a great company that stands the test of time is built.

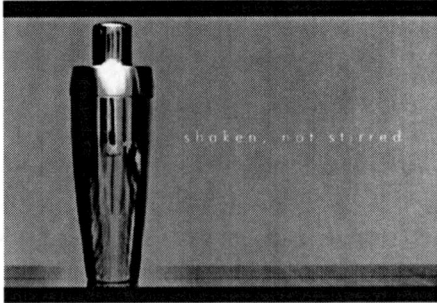

Brand strategy is the how, what, when, and to whom you plan on communicating your product or service. Having a clear and concise brand strategy leads to stronger overall brand equity -- how people feel about or perceive your product, and how much they are willing to pay for it.

It's the stuff that feels intangible, but it's that hard-to-pin-down feeling that separates powerhouse and mediocre brands from one another. So to help you rein in what many marketers consider more of an art and less of a science, we've broken down seven components of a comprehensive brand strategy that will help keep your company around for ages. So is your company's brand strategy smooth like Bond? Or will it leave your company shaken harder than Bond's martini?

Tie Your Brand to Your Business Model

Let's clear up the biggest misconception about brand strategy right now. Your brand is not your product, your logo, your website, or your name. It's what your customers perceive about you, and how you make them feel. Chances are you're not the only company out there selling your product or service. Figure out what your company does best beyond what you sell, and make it a part of your brand strategy.

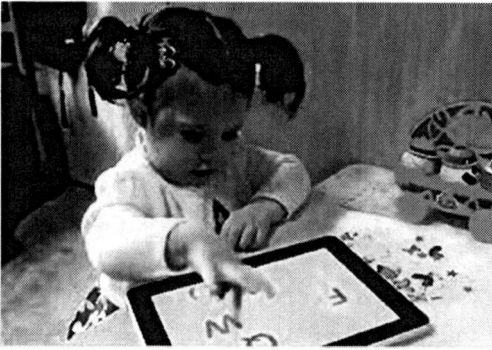

For example, Apple doesn't just sell computers and music equipment; it sells well-designed products that are easy to use. Are they the best computers on the market? No. (Well, I guess that depends on what side of the Mac-PC debate you're on.) But Apple sells a lot of them at twice the price because of the way Apple positions its brand in the market. This goes beyond your product itself -- it's about selling the problem you are solving.

Don't claim to solve generic problems; your customers have specific problems. Play the word game. Volvo = safe; Coke

= refreshing; Disney = magic; HubSpot = All-in-One. What does your brand equal? You always knew Bond was going to get out of a pickle, but you wanted to see howbecause he did it with resourcefulness and flair. Decide which aspect is the most important about your product or service, and make it a part of every aspect of your brand communication.

Be Consistent

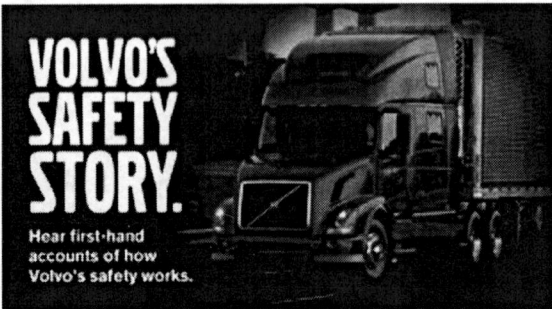

Now that you have decided your key brand attributes, make sure it is clear and understood through all your communications -- especially inside your own company. Don't talk about things that don't relate to or enhance your brand. Added a new photo to Facebook? What does it mean for your company? Does it align with your message, or was it just something funny that would, frankly, confuse your audience? If it doesn't tie back to your brand's message, you will have trouble differentiating yourself from competitors.

To reinforce the message, in your company meetings, over coffee or lunch, or just chatting at your desk, encourage the feelings you want your brand to evoke in customers and youremployees. When employees start to talk the talk and walk the walk -- especially those on the front lines -- the messaging is consistently reinforced with leads and customers, too.

You might be thinking, "Volvo doesn't say safety, safety, safety all the time, though." But listen to how Volvo describes its cars and how long they last, as well as how it describes features. It all ties back to Volvo's underlying brand theme of safety, and customers know what they will get when they buy that product.

Connect Emotionally

Customers can either think rationally about your product or service, or they can think emotionally about it. How else do you explain the person who paid thousands of dollars more for a Harley rather than buying another cheaper, equally well-made bike? There was an emotional voice in there somewhere, whispering "Buy a Harley...open road...tough." It's the way the brand makes youfeel. You feel like you belong, like you're part of a larger group that's more tight-knit than just a bunch of motorcycle riders. Where do you think HOG came from? Harley Owners Group.

Find a way to connect to your customers on a deeper level. Do you give them peace of mind? Make them feel like part of the family? Do you make life easier? Connect with your customers on this point before and after a sale. Answer their questions and concerns on social media. A little goes a long way. Batman doesn't have any real superpowers, but whenever that signal lights up the sky, people trust that he will be there -- because he always is.

Reward and Cultivate

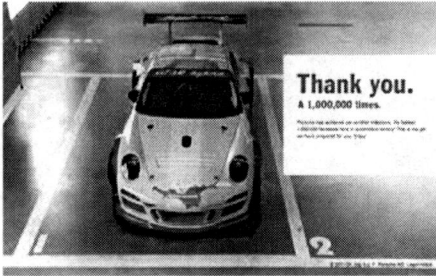

If you already have people that love you, your company, and your brand, don't just sit there! Reward them for that love. These customers have gone out their way to write about you, to tell their friends about you, and to act as your brand ambassadors. Cultivating loyalty from these people early on will yield more returning customers -- and more profit for your business.

Sometimes, just a thank you is all that's needed, but great brands also tend to give more than that. Write them a personalized letter. Do you have some extra special swag? Sent it to them. Ask them to write a review, and feature them prominently on your website. For example, Porsche reached 1 million Facebook fans quicker than any other automotive brand, so to thank its fans, Porsche made a wraparound for its GT3 Hybrid that included all 1 million names. No doubt the car company also received an extra bit of buzz for it. And showing how happy your current customers are with your product certainly helps your sales organization, too, because it shows the positive end result of becoming a customer.

Measure

Just because you come up with a campaign to reinforce your brand strategy, doesn't mean it will work. There have been plenty of schemes and plans that have ended with our beloved heroes in the clutches of an evil foe. How the Penguin catches anyone, I don't know, but if it can happen to Batman, it can happen to you. Watch your return on investment as you implement new campaigns to strengthen your brand. If your brand isn't resonating with enough people through the campaign, you have not given them a good enough reason to love you.

At the start of each new campaign, check your marketing analytics for branded and organic search. If it goes up when you launch your campaign, it means people are hearing about your campaign and becoming interested in your brand. They are searching for you -- often by name -- because you have provided them with enough compelling content that they want to know more. Just don't get stuck on one tactic or campaign. By staying agile, you can better measure whether your tactics are aligning well with your overall brand strategy, and if they don't, you haven't invested so much that you can't re-evaluate.

Be Flexible

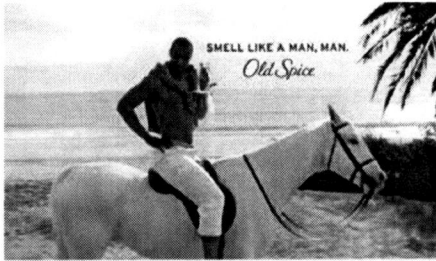

Speaking of agile inbound marketing, in this fast-changing world, marketers must remain flexible to stay relevant. On the plus side, this frees you to be creative with your campaigns. Old Spice generated quite the buzz over the last few years because it took its old brand and made it relatable to a new generation. Old Spice still held true to its brand; they just did it in a different, buzz-worthy way that opened them to a new customer market. I'm still talking about them, and that horse left the barn over a year ago.

So if your old tactics aren't working anymore, don't be afraid to change them just because it worked in the past. Take the opportunity to engage your followers in fresh, new ways. Are there some out-of-the-box partnerships your brand can make? Are there attributes about your product you never highlighted? Use those to connect with new customers and remind your old ones why they love you.

Watch Out for Competitors...a Little

Take the competition as a challenge to improve your own strategy and create greater value in your overall brand. You are in the same business and going after the same customers, right? So watch what they do. Do some of their tactics succeed? Do some fail? Tailor your tactics based on their experience to better your brand and company. For too many years, American car companies ignored their foreign competitors. But they finally realized they needed to change their model for the changing times and tout a more fuel-efficient agenda to keep pace with foreign competitors.

That being said, don't let your competitors dictate each and every move. I started this blog post talking about why you're in business. Sure, you probably sell a similar product or service as many other companies. But you're in business because your brand is unique. By harping on every move your competitor makes, you lose that differentiation. And soon your customers won't be able to tell you apart, making it even easier for them to leave you. Keep your eye on your competitors when experimenting with your brand strategy -- just not a hawk's eye.

What are some ways you evaluate the effectiveness of your brand strategy?

http://www.entrepreneur.com/article/77408

http://blog.hubspot.com/blog/tabid/6307/bid/31739/7-Components-That-Comprise-a-Comprehensive-Brand-Strategy.aspx

8

Direct Marketing

Direct marketing is about making direct contact with existing and potential customers to promote your products or services. Unlike media advertising, it enables you to target particular people with a personalised message. Direct marketing can be cost effective and extremely powerful at generating sales, so it is ideal for small businesses.

Direct marketing uses a variety of different methods. Direct mail, mailshots and leafleting are widespread, and other forms of direct and integrated communication are growing in popularity. Telephone marketing, mobile marketing, email and texting offer more opportunities to reach your target market.

Why use direct marketing?

Direct marketing allows you to generate a response from targeted customers. As a result, small businesses can focus their limited marketing resources where they are most likely to get results.

A direct marketing campaign with a clear call to action can help you boost your sales to existing customers, increase customer loyalty, recapture old customers and generate new business.

Direct marketing can be evaluated and measured precisely. You can analyse results to see which target group was most responsive. You can also test your marketing with sample groups before you roll out the campaign that will deliver the best response rate.

Whether you are targeting business (b2b) customers or consumers, direct marketing can deliver results. Choosing the right communication method is vital. Businesses can be more receptive to receiving sales calls than consumers, for example. Individuals will prefer different ways of contact, so make sure you take account of their preferences.

Getting the most out of your direct marketing campaign

Your database is at the heart of any good direct marketing strategy. It must be up to date and accurate. Check your mailing lists regularly - remove duplicate entries, correct any mistakes and, above all, delete names of people and businesses who have asked to be removed.

The information you hold on your database is marketing gold dust. It can tell you about your customers' buying habits and reveal other useful information such as age, gender and location. You can use this data to divide your customers and prospects into smaller groups and target them with special messages. You can build a profile of your best customers and actively seek new contacts matching that description by buying or renting new lists.

Direct marketing works because it puts your message in front of people. However, unsolicited letters, phone calls, faxes, emails and texts must only be sent to people and businesses that have given permission to be contacted. The Data Protection Act is complex and privacy laws are becoming tighter. It is your responsibility to check that your direct marketing activities are within the law.

Measuring the results of direct marketing

Whereas it can be difficult to measure the effects of advertising or sponsorship, in contrast, direct marketing is totally accountable. With any direct marketing campaign, you can calculate a break-even point - the number of sales you need to make to cover the cost of the marketing. In addition, you can work out the cost per response and the actual return on investment.

This simple analysis will enable you to tweak your campaigns in order to improve your results. You can also identify those that are most responsive and target them again in future.

http://www.marketingdonut.co.uk/marketing/direct-marketing

How To Do Direct Marketing That's Not Annoying

IRA KALB

MARSHALL SCHOOL OF BUSINESS, USC

Paramount Pictures

Ever since the World Wide Web began to be commercialized in 1995, the center of gravity in the marketing universe seems to have shifted toward the Internet and, more recently, social media and mobile devices.

The problem for marketers is how to effectively use these tools to develop brand relationships and sell products. Many marketers seem lost, and one of the reasons is that they have not learned how these new tools fit into the marketing strategy hierarchy.

Those that have achieved considerable success have recognized that the Internet and its "offspring" are really forms of Direct Marketing. Why? Because Direct Marketing channels are where buyers and sellers can transact business (and communicate) without ever meeting face-to-face or touching and feeling the merchandise. To make more effective use of these new tools, marketers need to become better educated in the concepts of Direct Marketing. The most commonly recognized Direct Marketing methods in historical order of discovery are:

1. Direct Mail,

2. Telemarketing,

3. Direct Response Advertising,

4. Internet, or online, marketing.

Direct Mail

In the United States, the roots of Direct Marketing can be traced to Benjamin Franklin who used Direct Mail to market Poor Richard's Almanac throughout the American colonies starting in 1732. Direct Mail continued to flourish with the creation of the Montgomery Ward catalog in 1872 and the Sears catalog in 1888. These catalogs were popular since a large segment of the American population lived outside of cities and towns that had stores with sufficient product choices.

As more people migrated to cities and suburbs, direct mail became popular for those that wanted to shop anonymously or could not easily travel to available stores. In its best form, Direct Mail provides a convenient way for prospects to receive information about products they want and order them without leaving the comfort of their home or office. In it's worst form, organizations send unwanted mailings to people that are not interested in the products being promoted. Of course, unwanted mailings are also known as "junk" mail, and their electronic equivalent is called "spam."

Telemarketing

Some might argue that telemarketing began with the invention of the telephone, but marketers began to use it on a significant scale in the late 1970's with the introduction of WATS lines for economically calling out to prospective customers and toll-free numbers for prospects to call in without paying for the call. This created the two main components of telemarketing – (1) Inbound (toll-free numbers are provided for customers to call in) and (2) Outbound (telemarketers call prospects). In its best form, companies use outbound telemarketing to answer questions, provide customer service, facilitate the ordering of desired products, and cross-selling (or upselling). In its most hated form, strangers "cold call" prospects, interrupt what they are doing, and try to sell them something they do not want. Some uses of outbound telemarketing became so annoying that a law was passed creating a Do Not Call Registry. Even so, outbound telemarketing can be very effective under the following conditions:

1. Prospect has given prior permission or wants the company to call,

2. Product is highly desirable or greatly needed,

3. Telemarketer is skillful and properly trained,

4. Telemarketer listens to the desires of the people that answer the phone (rather than try to keep them on the line when they want to end the call).

Direct Response Advertising

Direct Response Advertising is advertising with a goal of getting the prospect to order the product directly from the ad. Some examples of direct response advertising are a direct mail piece with a postage-paid business reply card that is used to order the product, a TV ad that provides a toll-free phone number to order, and an email that provides a link to order the product from a Web site.

Internet

Perhaps the method that has caused the most explosive growth of Direct Marketing is Internet marketing. There are two main reasons for this – (1) convenience and (2) economics. Even though the Internet is only a "teenager" (in reference to the beginning of its commercial use in 1995), nothing is more convenient or economical than the Internet for researching and ordering products. Even so, those that are using the Internet and related mobile technologies for marketing would be far more effective if they better understood the other Direct Marketing methods described above. Knowing how to use the Internet and its mobile "offspring" in conjunction with direct mail, telemarketing, and direct response advertising can create a synergistic force for marketing products most efficiently and effectively. Some people live online and some people don't. Those that live on the Internet may not be online when a company needs to get their attention.

Additionally, repetition of the information off-line helps them remember any exposure online. Similarly, those that spend most of their time off-line, can learn more about products when off-line marketing drives them online. A poster in a shopping mall, a direct mail post card with a coupon, or a display in a retail store may get their attention. If these offline devices have a link or QR code, prospects can be transported to a Web site that gives them the opportunity to find out more about the product, helps them find where they can buy it, and enables them to order it directly. Taking this integration of direct marketing methods further by combining them with other off-line marketing methods can give marketers the greatest power at the lowest cost.

Direct Marketing can lower sales costs

Lowering the costs of personal selling is one example of how integrated Direct Marketing is used with other forms of marketing. In a previous post, I talked about the importance of personal selling to success in business. When it comes to promoting products, however, personal selling is also one of the most expensive methods in a marketer's toolkit. According to the latest studies by McGraw-Hill, it costs an average of $589.18 for one industrial sales call. Since it takes roughly 5 calls to close a deal, the cost of closing a sale averages roughly $3,000. That might work for selling airplanes and satellite systems or million-dollar clients. It would be too expensive selling many other products. That's the bad news. The good news is that sales people can use the Internet and other Direct Marketing techniques for some (or even all) of the calls – thereby lowering overall sales costs. Most of my business opportunities overseas have been initiated, developed, and closed via Direct Marketing.

Social media

As discussed above, just about everyone is talking about using social media in marketing products. The problem is too many don't know how to effectively do it. While "earned media" techniques such as hauling represent very exciting new ways for promoting products, most of them are experimental and outside the control of your business. In an effort to take advantage of social media without ceding too much control, marketers need to have some understanding of popular social media channels and how to integrate them with other Direct Marketing methods.

• Facebook has a large number of active users (over 1 Billion at last count) and a lot of data on users so that advertisers can better target them. Since people go to Facebook to interact with friends and family, they do not like intrusions from companies. However, a lot of friends and family recommend products on Facebook, and company pages are very popular places for prospects to learn about products, discover new uses, find discounts, and share all this with their friends. At the very least, Facebook can make more brand impressions than other media. Companies pay $3 million for the opportunity to reach roughly 110 million Super Bowl viewers one day a year. On Facebook, they have potential to reach a much larger audience at a much lower cost every day of the week. While Facebook limits ad sizes to very small spaces so as not to ruin user experiences, good marketers can make effective use of the space allotted with concise headlines.

• Twitter is great for those that know how to write good headlines since it limits users to 140 characters. While it accounts for much less Web traffic than Facebook and other social media, Twitter users tend to be more influential. Also, Twitter can easily be linked to other SM sites, such as Facebook, so that if you post on Twitter, your Tweet can automatically appear on Facebook simultaneously. Twitter has proven to be very effective in responding to complaints, rumors, and factual mistakes for damage control and to provide better customer service. Companies that have learned to use Twitter in this way have been able to "turn negatives into positives" and build closer relationships with their constituents.

• YouTube provides a place for companies large and small to reach their target audience without paying the high "real estate" costs of commercial TV channels. Furthermore, YouTube videos can be shared, and if they go viral, the numbers of viewers that actually watch the commercial can rival and even surpass TV audiences. YouTube viewers can also play the videos over and over again as well as share them with even larger networks of viewers enabling advertisers to make more brand impressions and greater sales.

• Linked In is good for business markets. The HR departments of businesses use it to find candidates, and businesses can put profiles of their products and white papers on the site, and use it to promote their business. According to Linked In, 43% of marketers have found a customer on Linked In during 2013

Integrating Social Media

To increase the marketing power of social media, marketers should be sure to integrate it with all other direct and non-direct channels. Direct mail, telemarketing, and direct response advertising should have links to social media, and vice versa. A lot of companies ask market targets to visit their Web site and "like" or "follow" them on social media, but too often they do not provide the benefit for doing so. Similarly, social media rarely ties campaigns to off-line and other direct marketing efforts – missing opportunities for marketing synergy, making additional brand impressions, and increasing sales. Companies with effective campaigns have linked product packaging and off-line media to social and online media. In addition to asking people to "like" or "follow" or visit social media and Web sites, they have given people codes in traditional media and on product packaging that give those that make the effort a chance to win a prize, learn something, or save money. The feedback and contact information provided is more than worth the costs of the prize, rebate, or discount, and gives the company a chance to improve the product or add contact information to their database.

Advergaming

Some companies have successfully used Advergaming as a way to tie their media efforts together. When it works best, users have to go online and off for clues that teach them about the benefits of the products and company. They have fun while they are learning, are engaged, and remember the benefits. As a result, brand impressions and reasons to buy the products are better planted in the brains of prospects.

The power of Direct Marketing

Direct marketing has grown in power for a variety of factors that include the following.

1. Less time. Market targets are busier than ever before since they have to work harder to earn a living.

2. Less hassles and dangers. Increasing traffic, parking costs, and other hassles have reduced the desire for buyers to go to retail stores to do their shopping.

3. Less expensive. The costs of buying and marketing products in "non-direct" ways has skyrocketed at the same time that financial disruptions, natural disasters, and government dysfunction has forced buyers to become more frugal.

4. More convenient. The Internet is perhaps the most convenient way for buyers to research products, comparison shop, and order from their home, office, or mobile device.

5. Anonymous. Some buyers prefer shopping for certain products anonymously.

Based on these economic and convenience factors, Direct Marketing is likely to continue to grow rapidly. Marketers that better understand Direct Marketing and how to integrate its various components into a synergistic mix of marketing strategies are likely to reap the benefits. And, the benefits are substantial since the Direct Marketing Association estimates that Direct Marketing produced $2.05 trillion in sales in 2012 - representing roughly 8.7% if US GDP (Gross Domestic Product).

http://www.businessinsider.com/the-exploding-importance-of-direct-marketing-2013-11#ixzz31t6OyEVK

http: //www.businessinsider.com/the-exploding-importance-of-direct-marketing-2013-11

Strategies for direct marketing

Tim Berry

Are you getting the most from your direct marketing? Make sure your direct marketing campaigns are target, measurable, and ethical.

About Direct Marketing

As we discussed in Direct Marketing Fudamentals, direct marketing includes various approaches in which the producer of goods or services directly contacts the end-user. Direct marketing encompasses face-to-face selling, direct mail, catalogs, kiosks, telemarketing, and more. Regardless of the form you choose, there are some critical considerations.

Targeted Campaigns

The criteria for direct marketing begins with a reliable customer database. Other factors include offering greater customer value through a more customized and personalized approach for product and service offerings, distribution processes tailored to meet the needs of customers, and the opportunity to build customer loyalty.

One of the first criteria for direct marketing is to have a consistent customer profile available which describes the dominant target markets. This information must have sufficient detail to support a customer database.

A customer database quantitatively captures the key characteristics of prospects and customers who are most ready, willing, and able to purchase your product or service. It may offer demographic information about their age, income, education, gender, and previous mail order purchases. In concert with this information, this customer database identifies customers who possess these characteristics:

• Have purchased most frequently

• Purchased recently

• Spend the most at each transaction

This database is used to accomplish the following.

• Identify prospects

• Decide when a customer needs a specific offer.

• Enhance customer loyalty

• Stimulate repeat purchases

Access to a customer database is the first step. The next set of criteria includes enhancing customer value through one or more of the following factors:

• Customized product and service solutions

• Personalized interaction before or during the actual transaction

• The development of expertise within an industry or based on specific issues

• Individualized distribution processes accompanied by customized marketing offerings

When these criteria are met, the organization may be able to leverage areas of expertise, economies of scale, and have the potential to build customer loyalty. An organization may be able to achieve greater target market precision through direct marketing than it can experience through a mass marketing or channel marketing approach.

Before You Begin, Decide How to Measure

Successful direct marketing campaigns plan their efforts, determine their objectives, target their markets, determine the offers' key elements, test those elements, and establish measurements to assess the campaign's success. Measuring your success is key.

Begin by gathering information about your fixed costs relating to overhead expenses and the variable costs relating to how many pieces are going to be sent. Then prepare to track revenues generated. Each of these areas offers valuable information to assess the results of the direct marketing campaign.

Conducting a simple break-even analysis can be a valuable tool in this process. For example:

Dental Data Co. is an organization that offers specialized patient management software to dentists. They would like to determine what their break-even point would be if they mailed CD-ROM demos with printed materials to 2,000 selected dentists. Their estimated expenses for the direct mail campaign follow.

This information will help determine what Dental Data's response rate needs to be to break even on the campaign. The 43 units to break-even equates to a 2.15% response rate. This response rate is determined by dividing the 43 units at break-even by 2,000, the total number mailed.

Therefore, if Dental Data does not have a response rate higher than 2.15% over the time period they have determined, they will not realize profit from this direct marketing effort.

You can test the anticipated response rate, based on establishing a break-even sales point, to better understand the possible combinations of potential results. Information regarding general direct mail response rates, industry standards, or your past direct marketing experiences may be used to predict reasonable response rates.

Analyzing your direct marketing campaign can allow you to steadily improve direct marketing performance. If multiple direct mail pieces are used, analyze the response rates from each.

This measurement may consider the results that occur after the conclusion of the campaign. Some direct marketing campaigns produce results months or years after the campaign has been assessed. Initial "failure" may change into a successful campaign if results are tracked and measured over time.

Ethical Considerations and Responsibilities

Not all marketing is good marketing. It is important to recognize that some direct marketing techniques contain negative attributes that impact the targeted group. This may include invasion of privacy, deception, or fraud.

Invasion of privacy issues are often associated with telemarketing. How many long distance provider calls have you received in the middle of dinner? "Spam" email messages sent to numerous computer mail addresses clutter inboxes. How many are you receiving each day? These activities can create negative impact on a potential customer, and cost money that could be more effectively spent elsewhere.

Direct marketing can also involve using communication vehicles that exaggerate information and mislead buyers through deceptive claims about a product size, performance, or price. Products that fail to meet the claim, and nonprofit organizations that use funds for other purposes, are guilty of inaccurate or misleading direct mail promotion tactics. In addition to creating a negative image, this kind of marketing can be legally risky.

Consider the potential ramifications a direct marketing campaign may have on your product, service, and organization when selecting, designing, and implementing the campaign.

http://www.mplans.com/articles/strategies-for-direct-marketing/

9

<u>SALES PROMOTION</u>

Basic Definitions: Advertising, Marketing, Promotion, Public Relations and Publicity.

DISCUSSION IN 'SALES, MARKETING & PR' STARTED BY IINFOTECH10, JUL 30, 2010.

It's easy to become confused about these terms: advertising, marketing, promotion, public relations and publicity, and sales. The terms are often used interchangeably. However, they refer to different -- but similar activities. Some basic definitions are provided below. A short example is also provided hopefully to help make the terms more clear to the reader.

One Definition of Advertising

Advertising is bringing a product (or service) to the attention of potential and current customers. Advertising is focused on one particular product or service. Thus, an advertising plan for one product might be very different than that for another product. Advertising is typically done with signs, brochures, commercials, direct mailings or e-mail messages, personal contact, etc.

One Definition of Promotion

Promotion keeps the product in the minds of the customer and helps stimulate demand for the product. Promotion involves ongoing advertising and publicity (mention in the press). The ongoing activities of advertising, sales and public relations are often considered aspects of promotions.

One Definition of Marketing

Marketing is the wide range of activities involved in making sure that you're continuing to meet the needs of your customers and getting value in return. Marketing is usually focused on one product or service. Thus, a marketing plan for one product might be very different than that for another product. Marketing activities include "inbound marketing," such as market research to find out, for example, what groups of potential customers exist, what their needs are, which of those needs you can meet, how you should meet them, etc. Inbound marketing also includes analyzing the competition, positioning your new product or service (finding your market niche), and pricing your products and services. "Outbound marketing" includes promoting a product through continued advertising, promotions, public relations and sales.

One Definition of Public relations

Public relations includes ongoing activities to ensure the overall company has a strong public image. Public relations activities include helping the public to understand the company and its products. Often, public relations are conducted through the media, that is, newspapers, television, magazines, etc. As noted above, public relations is often considered as one of the primary activities included in promotions.

One Definition of Publicity

Publicity is mention in the media. Organizations usually have little control over the message in the media, at least, not as they do in advertising. Regarding publicity, reporters and writers decide what will be said.

One Definition of Sales

Sales involves most or many of the following activities, including cultivating prospective buyers (or leads) in a market segment; conveying the features, advantages and benefits of a product or service to the lead; and closing the sale (or coming to agreement on pricing and services). A sales plan for one product might be very different than that for another product.

http://www.ukbusinessforums.co.uk/threads/basic-definitions-advertising-marketing-promotion-public-relations-and-publicity.166292/

SALES PROMOTION ADVERTISING

Sales promotion is, in its simplest form, any brand initiative designed to promote sales, usage or trial of products, leading to a measurable direct impact of the number of sales.

Sales promotion is best thought of as an umbrella term, incorporating numerous forms of promotions, from money off voucher or coupons, to on-pack promotions and everything else in-between. The primary focus of sales promotion advertising is to positively impact on sales, and is very efficient at doing so, but it can also impact on wider elements of your marketing strategy, working to drive loyalty to the brand itself, through communication and demonstration, giving consumers a much better idea of your brand, it's products and the quality of these products ahead of making any purchase. Sales promotion can also be utilised to drive consumers to separate channels, whether this is driving to Facebook, Twitter or other sites within the social space, to search, promoting offers through specific brand-coined terms and phrases, and indeed, driving to the brand's website itself.

WHAT ELEMENTS DOES AN EFFECTIVE SALES PROMOTION CAMPAIGN NEED TO HAVE?

Some of the common objectives of a sales promotion advertising campaign include product trial, brand loyalty and increased frequency of sales, all of which are metrics which through sales promotion are easy to detract and measure, making sales promotion marketing one or the more accountable and transparent elements of a marketing strategy. This ability to measure with ease the impact sales promotion advertising has on your sales is what makes it so attractive to marketers, as the returns of this activity can be readily quantified, demonstrating its benefit to your sales figures with ease, making sales promotion advertising a definite must in today's economic climate.

A frequent feature of sales promotion advertising is the use of associations between the brand and celebrities, films, events or even other brands, working in conjunction with one another to appeal to consumers interests beyond your products and services.

This makes your communications better received, appealing to users by demonstrating that your brand is the best for them, making them believe that due to these associations that your brand is the best choice for their lifestyle. There are numerous examples of well executed sales promotion advertising campaigns that utilise such associations, with those of note include McDonald's, who associated with kids movie releases with their Happy Meal product, Carlsberg's association with the England football team and Robinson's on-pack promotions for the Wimbledon tennis championship. When deciding to draw such associations with your brand it is important to get it right, remaining mindful of the negative impact the wrong association could have for your brand and the subsequent impact this could have on your sales promotion advertising.

WHICH TYPES OF PROMOTION FALL UNDER THE SALES PROMOTION BANNER?

Types of sales promotion activities that are commonly utilised in such campaigns can include prize draws and competitions, free mail, purchase gifts, liquidating promotions and, in its most simply form, discounts and vouchers. The means and methodology employed in the execution of a good sales promotion advertising campaign has changed in recent years, with this change being due to the advent of new media from the digital real, most notably the surge in social media and networking. A sales promotion campaign which is mindful of and designed to best utilise this will yield far better results and is essential for sales promotion advertising in the world in which we live today.

WHY SHOULD I HAVE SALES PROMOTION IN MY MARKETING STRATEGY?

Put simply, sales promotion advertising provides consumers with an additional incentive or reason to make a purchase beyond the product itself. This can be something as simple as a prize draw, loyalty reward or discount on their next order, ensuring that consumers are driven back to your brand over those of you competitors time and time again.

10

ADVERTISING

Principles of Effective Advertising

The first step

An advertising strategy includes four elements:

1. target audience

2. product/service concept

3. communications media

4. advertising message

Five elements of ads

1. Attention – the headline should act as a stimulus and cut through the clutter. It must be appropriate, relating to the product or service, the tone of the ad, and the needs or interests of the intended audience.

2. Interest – keeps the prospects involved as the information becomes more detailed.

3. Credibility – makes believable claims.

4. Desire – describes the benefits of the product or service.

5. Action – motivates people to do something, such as call or visit a website

Principles of design

1. Use simple layouts.

2. Headlines are short, powerful, and to the point, and the image tells the story quickly.

3. Does not use dense, lengthy blocks of ad copy.

4. Design ads with optimal flow – we read from top to bottom and left to right. Ads that make the reader fight this natural tendency lower comprehension.

5. Photos are generally most effective compared to illustration.

6. Whenever possible, show action or a product in use (rather than a static shot).

Writing effective copy

1. Get to the main point – fast.

2. Emphasize one major idea simply and clearly.

3. Be single-minded. Don't try to do too much. Position the product or service clearly.

4. Write short sentences. Use easy, familiar words and themes people understand.

5. Write from the reader's point of view. Avoid "we," "us," "our."

6. Use personal pronouns, such as "you" and "your."

7. Use vivid language. Stick to the present tense, active voice.

8. Use contractions.

9. Don't overpunctuate.

10. Never write negative copy – positive copy gets better results.

11. Humour is tricky and its effectiveness can wear out after two or three exposures. Humour generally does not work with business or professional audiences.

12. Use technical language sparingly, unless essential to reach your audience.

13. Use bold subheads and numbered/bulleted lists to break up the sea of type.

14. Vary sentence length. One-word sentences and sentence fragments are acceptable.

15. Avoid extremely long lines of type (65 characters per line or more).

Frequency

• The higher the price, the higher the frequency needs. Research has shown that brands with longer purchase cycles are likely to benefit from higher frequencies of exposure.

• An image ad, a new campaign or a complicated message requires more frequency.

• Weak advertising will not work no matter what the frequency.

• With any multi-media campaign, make sure the creative is synergistic (the same look and feel across all media).

• Advertising is most effective when a person is in the market to buy.

• Messages have the greatest effect when they are received close to purchase.

Size, colour and positioning

• The more the size of an ad increases, the more people notice an ad.

• Buying almost a page (70-90% of a page) does not appear as effective as buying a full page.

• Ad noting increases with colour – using full colour increases ad noting by 34% (except in a publication where all the ads are colour).

• Ads in a vertical format are noted somewhat more.

• The larger the picture, the more an ad is noticed.

• Overall, there is no difference between right and left pages.

• Ads on the bottom of the page are noted slightly more than those on the top.

• In most sections, banner ads on the front page of a section are read more than banner ads inside the section.

http://www.bcit.ca/marcom/brand/adprinciples.shtml

10 Principles Of Advertising

Bill Bernbach

1. Go to the essence of the product. State the product's essence in the simplest terms of its basic advantage. And state this both tangibly and memorably.

2. Where possible, make your product an actor in the scene; not just a prop. This makes for a tremendously effective method of getting your product remembered. Because the provocative element in your advertising is also the element that sells your product. This is so simply stated, so difficult to execute.

3. Art and copy must be fully integrated. They must be conceived as a unit, developed as a unit.

4. Advertising must have vitality. This exuberance is sometimes called "personality". When advertising has a personality, it is persuasively different; and it is the one because of the other. You must fight to get "bounce" in your advertising.

5. It is little less than useless to employ a so-called gimmick in advertising —- unless the gimmick itself tells the product story.

6. Tell the truth. First, it's a great gimmick. Second, you go to heaven. Third, it moves merchandise because people will trust you.

7. Be relevant. A wonderfully creative execution will get the big "So what" if it isn't meaningful to their life, family, business etc. And always opt for an ad that's relevant over one that's exciting and irrelevant.

8. Be simple. Not simpleminded, but single minded. Who has the time or the desire to listen to advertising?

9. Safe ideas can kill you. If it's been done before, your competition will be ready for it. Your only chance of beating the competition is with advertising they've never seen before. Which means you've never seen it before either! Be brave.

10. Stand out. If your advertising goes unnoticed, everything has been wasted.

Timeless advice by Advertising Legend Bill Bernbach.

http://www.brandingstrategyinsider.com/2010/10/10-principles-of-advertising-bill-bernbach.html#.U3YnnfldXXk

Basic Principles of Advertising

Sell people things but always buy their friendship – Sir Naeem

Introduction

Advertising is the business of drawing public attention to goods and services. When you begin to create advertising for your product or service, keep these suggestions in mind:

1. Don't make promises you can't live up to. Although your ad may draw more people to your product initially, you can't retain these people as loyal customers in the long run if you make promises you can't keep.

2. Identify the best features of whatever it is you're selling and develop your advertising around these features. Think about how your product stands out from the competition, what sets it apart, and then focus on those attributes.

3. Try to create a memorable advertising message for your product. You want people to think of your store, your product, or your professional service whenever they're in the market for such a thing.

The Message of Advertising

If your message is creative, clear, and concise, if your product or service issomething that can truly benefit people and live up to its hype, then you'reon the road to producing effective advertising. If your advertising makes bold promises about your product, you may convince a lot of people to try it. But if those people buy your product and give it a try, and the product turns out to be less than you advertised it to be, you will most certainly never see those consumers again. Think about it: How many times have you responded to an advertising message for a new, improved, astounding product, only to be disappointed with the item after you tried it? You probably even felt like you'd been ripped off. If your advertising message leaves consumers with the same feeling, you simply won't get anywhere. One good promise on which you can truly deliver is better than trying to be all things to all people. On the average, five times as many people read the headline as read the body copy. When you have written your headline, you have spent 80 cents out of your dollar. Never write an advertisement you wouldn't want your own family to read. You wouldn't tell lies to your own wife. Don't tell lies to mine. In advertising, every word in the copy must count you sell or else. Advertise only what is unique.

Identifying and Targeting Your Audience

To begin the creative process of finding your one-of-a-kind message and understand your audience, ask yourself a few simple questions:

1. What are you selling, and what makes it so unique? For example, if you need to sell kids toys, what makes your merchandise different from what people can buy from other big retail chains? Are the toys handmade, imported from other countries, or vintage?

2. To whom do you want to sell it? In other words, who exactly are you targeting as your ideal consumer? Parents, of course, but what type of parent? Do you want to target wealthy, upscale parents, who are most interested in educational games that will help their kids learn, for example? You may also think about marketing to aunts, uncles, and grandparents, who often want

to spend more on their nieces, nephews, and grandchildren than the parents do.

3. Why should people buy the product or service from you? Are you open very late at night so that parents who work long hours can drop by your store? Do you offer free delivery of large items so that walk-in customers don't have to lug your product home? Are you (and your staff) especially knowledgeable and approachable about suggesting great toys for different age groups?

Words that Sell

Certain words and phrases, when used in advertising, have a better-than-everchance of attracting consumers' attention. You see these words over andover again in ads, but their overuse is a direct result of their effectiveness.

Different words or phrases work for different types of businesses, though.

Here are some examples of words and phrases that sell in the retail industry:

1. Clearance

2. Discount

3. Everything must go

4. Final closeout

5. Free

6. Going out of business

7. Grand opening

The challenge lies in walking a fine line between using simple, easy-to-grasp words and phrases and writing the way people think (in everyday conversational English). Bottom line: Make your ads simple in their language but creative in their content and presentation. If you offer a service instead of providing a product, many of the words from the previous list still work. "Free," for example, always gets consumers' attention, as does "new." The following appealing words and phrases, however, are specific to the service industry:

1. Great service

2. Free pickup and delivery

3. On time

4. Trial offer

5. Professional

6. Family owned and operated

7. Guaranteed service

8. Money saving

9. Dependable (or reliable)

10. High quality

11. References available from satisfied customers

Go through your newspaper and look at the ads. Certain words and phrasesused by most advertisers will quickly become apparent to you. Now youknow what I mean when I say that these words sell. They form a similarthread that runs through most advertising. If you can use any of these wordsand phrases in your advertising, by all means include them. If they're goodenough for the other advertisers in your area, they'll most certainly be goodenough for you.

Make an ad, not an encyclopedia

The primary mistake made in many print ads is verbosity. The philosophy seems to be: Why use 5 words when 500 words will do? Readers aren't interested in how to make a fine Swiss watch. They're only interested in how much money they can save if they buy the watch from you. A brief headline is particularly important. A headline reading, "50 PERCENT SAVINGS" is better than one reading, Everything storewide has been marked down 50 percent." Making your headline brief, intriguing, and easy to grasp, most certainly, enhances your ad's effectiveness. Trying to fit too much information into the headline can be self-defeating. Use the subhead or the body copy for the nuts and bolts of your sales pitch. Keep your body copy brief and your graphic elements relevant and bold. That way, you make it easy for your readers to grasp what you're trying to say and what you're striving to sell. Just because you've spent a fair amount of money to buy the ad space doesn't mean that you have to fill it wall-to-wall. An ad that's easy for the reader to understand may be rewarded with the reader dropping into your store or contacting you, credit card poised and at the ready! Do what I do: Write your ad, and then go back and see how many superfluous words you can eliminate until your copy is as tight as it can possibly be. In print copy, less is more!

Conclusion

Your advertising is like radios or TVs. They are there to get the attention of your listeners and viewers— people you want to become customers if they aren't already. Before you sit down and start writing, consider: If you want your ad to be effective, keep it short and following these final guidelines.

1. Grab the listeners' attention

2. Tell them something they want to hear

3. Sell them something they may not need

4. Mention the name of your business several times

5. Get your phone number or Web address indelibly written into their brains

6. Motivate them with a call to action (something that tells your reader what to do, such as "Call today for the best prices!" or "In stores now!")

You can also use Collateral advertising. It has numerous purposes — and the different kinds of collateral advertising at your disposal are numerous as well. You should research carefully, always keeping your budget in mind, to determine which form of collateral advertising best suits your needs. Types of collateral ads include: Brochures, Post cards, Business Cards and and Newsletters.

http://www.brandingstrategyinsider.com/2010/10/10-principles-of-advertising-bill-bernbach.html#.U3YnnfldXXk

11

<u>MARKET RESEARCH AND</u>
<u>ANALYSIS</u>

What Are the Principles of Market Research?

Thomas Gee, eHow Contributor

Organizations need market information to grow and better serve their consumers. Marketing research is the process by which organizations procure the information that enables better decision-making as they advance toward these goals.

1. Objectives

o All marketing research begins with an objective. An objective can be as simple as "Which formula for our soft-drink brand tastes best to our consumers?" or as complex as "What should be our five-year strategy for expanding our computer software brand into other categories?"

If a research objective is articulated effectively, other details of the project fall into place, including whom to talk to, what specific technique to use, what questions to ask and how the information will be used.

2. Sampling Plan

o Since it is impractical to talk with everyone whose opinion a firm might want, the organization instead speaks to a sample of those individuals, with the expectation that this sample will estimate the opinions of the entire population.

There are many sample-creation methods, and which is used depends on the objectives of a project. In general, larger samples are better: Although all samples entail error, with larger samples, error is reduced. You can then be more confident your sample measurements approximate those of your population.

3. Instrument

o Research instruments--that is, how the information is to be collected--will vary depending on the objective(s). In some cases, a qualitative approach might be sufficient, so a set of four focus groups might be appropriate. In other cases, a quantitative approach is needed, so you might need a survey to be answered by hundreds of people.

A simple rule of thumb is to determine whether the answer you seek is something that can be quantified. If so, you will likely field a quantitative-based survey with a large sample. You can also examine where you are in an overall project timeline. In early stages, frequently only guidance or preliminary information is needed, and therefore the research can be qualitative or smaller in scale. At later stages, when significant resource allocation decisions need to be made, larger quantitative research would likely be appropriate.

4. Action Standards

o Action standards (a.k.a. decision criteria) are the articulation of how the research will be used--specifically, what decision is being made with the research, and what criteria will be used to make that decision.

In many cases, it is helpful to have benchmarks. Sometimes, companies have their own internal benchmarks; at other times, research suppliers have historical benchmarks based on years of testing.

Let's say Company A is interested in replacing its current product with one of two potentially improved products, and plans to execute a test with users of the current product, where the current product is compared to the two potential improvements . Here, the current product is the benchmark, and the action standard could read that if one of the two new potential products significantly outscores the current product on a key measure, like preference, that new product would replace the current product.

5. Error and Risk

o No matter how well a marketing research test is designed and executed, there is always some risk the information you receive is faulty or even false, and therefore could lead you to make a wrong decision.

There are two basic types of risk. Looking at the Company A example above, there is a risk that if one of the new products outperforms the current product, the new product is actually inferior to the current product and should not be introduced. This risk is also referred to a "Type I error."

Conversely, if neither of the two new products outscores the current product, there is also a risk that one or both is actually superior to the current one, and should be introduced. This risk is also referred to as "Type II error."

Although it is impossible to eliminate, risk can be reduced, or at least managed. The easiest way to reduce both kinds of risk is to increase the sample size of a test. If one type is error is deemed more grievous than the other, an action standard can be manipulated so that type of error is minimized--but the trade-off will be that the other type of error will increase. In practice, most research tests seek to balance risk between the two types of errors.

6. Analysis

o The most basic analysis consists of simple descriptive statistics--that is, what percentage of people answered this way or that way to our questions. This output is frequently accompanied by significance testing. For example, in an advertising test with two new ads and a current ad as a benchmark, both new ads could be compared to the current on a measure such as viewer interest, with an action standard that an alternative ad will only be produced and broadcast if it outperforms the current ad on this measure at a 90 percent confidence level.

Another common analytic technique is cross-tabulating descriptive statistics. With this technique, you can examine subsets of interest-- such as men, households with children, or current brand users--and make comparison between them and to your total sample.

There are many more elaborate analytical techniques, such as regression, factor analysis and discriminant analysis. These tools are used less frequently, but can come into play depending on the research objectives.

7. Overall Design Considerations

o In designing marketing research, researchers must balance several factors and recommend the most appropriate research for the question at hand, the risk involved and, of course, the budget.

An important skill for a researcher is scaling a project appropriately. For example, if a brand wants to introduce a new flavor or size of an existing product, that is a far less risky proposition than if it wants to introduce a totally new product in a different category. The latter situation would likely call for a larger, more comprehensive test.

Factors that drive research cost include the sample size, the difficulty of recruiting the right people, the length of the survey, and the level of analysis required after the fact.

http://www.ehow.com/about_5132158_principles-market-research.html#ixzz31tPCTcHW

How to Do Market Research - The Basics

Lesley Spencer Pyle

Is your business a product in search of a customer? Use these tips to create a product or service customers will clamor for.

Marketing research can give a business a picture of what kinds of new products and services may bring a profit. For products and services already available, marketing research can tell companies whether they are meeting their customers' needs and expectations. By researching the answers to specific questions, small-business owners can learn whether they need to change their package design or tweak their delivery methods--and even whether they should consider offering additional services.

"Failure to do market research before you begin a business venture or during its operation is like driving a car from Texas to New York without a map or street signs," says William Bill of Wealth Design Group LLC in Houston. "You have know which direction to travel and how fast to go. A good market research plan indicates where and who your customers are. It will also tell you when they are most likely and willing to purchase your goods or use your services."

When you conduct marketing research, you can use the results either to create a business and marketing plan or to measure the success of your current plan. That's why it's important to ask the right questions, in the right way, of the right people. Research, done poorly, can steer a business in the wrong direction. Here are some market-research basics that can help get you started and some mistakes to avoid.

Types of Market Research

Primary Research: The goal of primary research is to gather data from analyzing current sales and the effectiveness of current practices. Primary research also takes competitors' plans into account, giving you information about your competition.

Collecting primary research can include:

• Interviews (either by telephone or face-to-face)

• Surveys (online or by mail)

• Questionnaires (online or by mail)

• Focus groups gathering a sampling of potential clients or customers and getting their direct feedback

Some important questions might include:

• What factors do you consider when purchasing this product or service?

• What do you like or dislike about current products or services currently on the market?

• What areas would you suggest for improvement?

• What is the appropriate price for a product or service?

Secondary Research: The goal of secondary research is to analyze data that has already been published. With secondary data, you can identify competitors, establish benchmarks and identify target segments. Your segments are the people who fall into your targeted demographic--people who live a certain lifestyle, exhibit particular behavioral patterns or fall into a predetermined age group.

Collecting Data

No small business can succeed without understanding its customers, its products and services, and the market in general. Competition is often fierce, and operating without conducting research may give your competitors an advantage over you.

There are two categories of data collection: quantitative and qualitative. Quantitative methods employ mathematical analysis and require a large sample size. The results of this data shed light on statistically significant differences. One place to find quantitative results if you have a website is in your web analytics (available in Google's suite of tools). This information can help you determine many things, such as where your leads are coming from, how long visitors are staying on your site and from which page they are exiting.

Qualitative methods help you develop and fine-tune your quantitative research methods. They can help business owners define problems and often use interview methods to learn about customers' opinions, values and beliefs. With qualitative research, the sample size is usually small.

Many new business owners, often strapped for time and money, may take shortcuts that can later backfire. Here are three pitfalls to avoid.

Common Marketing Mistakes

1. Using only secondary research. Relying on the published work of others doesn't give you the full picture. It can be a great place to start, of course, but the information you get from secondary research can be outdated. You can miss out on other factors relevant to your business.

2. Using only web resources. When you use common search engines to gather information, you get only data that are available to everyone and it may not be fully accurate. To

perform deeper searches while staying within your budget, use the resources at your local library, college campus or small-business center.

3. Surveying only the people you know. Small-business owners sometimes interview only family members and close colleagues when conducting research, but friends and family are often not the best survey subjects. To get the most useful and accurate information, you need to talk to real customers about their needs, wants and expectations.

Conducting Online Market Research:

Tips and Tools

INC. STAFF

How to use online market research tools, including search techniques, tips, and tools for using the Internet for researching your competition and market.

Your may already be conducting online market research for your business—but you may not know it. Some of the easiest to use and most common tools are located right at your fingertips. Web searches, online questionnaires, customer feedback forms—they all help you gather information about your market, your customers, and your future business prospects.

The advent of the Internet has presented small businesses with a wealth of additional resources to use in conducting free or low-cost market research. The following pages will describe the different types of tools to conduct online market research, go over the general categories of market research, and advise you how to create the best online questionnaires.

Online Market Research Tools

The following techniques can be used to gather market information with the help of a few mouse clicks and keystrokes:

• Keyword Search. You know how to do a simple Web search using search engines such as Google and Yahoo. Take that a step farther by searching for "keywords" that people would use to find your type of products or services on the Internet. See how much interest there is in these keywords -- and how many competitors you have in this market. Keyword searches can also help remind you of product niches that you might not have considered. There are other reasons to conduct keyword searches. 'First, you're going to be reminded of product niches that you might not of thought of.' says Jennifer Laycock, editor-in-chief of Search Engine Guide, an online guide to search engines, portals and directories. 'Second, these services will also give you a guesstimate of how many existing sites already use that phrase,' Laycock continues. 'How many existing sites already offer that product.' WordTracker and Trellian's Keyword Discovery are popular keyword search engines.

• Competitor Links. A traditional search engine can also help you check out your competitors, their prices, and their offerings. Try typing 'link:www.[competitor's name].com' into Google to find out how many other sites link to your competitor's website. 'It is a great way to see a competitor's link development and PR campaigns,' says Shari Thurow, Web expert and author of the upcoming book Search Engine Visibility. 'Is the competitor promoting a product or service similar to your own? Maybe you can get publicity because you have a new or better product.'

• Read Blogs. Blogs are updated much more regularly than traditional websites and, therefore, they can be another gauge of public opinion. Search blogs by using blog-specific search engines, such as Technorati or Nielsen BuzzMetrics' Blogpulse. 'Blogs tend to move at a faster pace and be more informal in tone, so you're more likely to pick up conversation about a new product type or need on a blog than on a standard web site,' Laycock says.

• Conduct Online Surveys. Another way to gauge public opinion is through online surveys. While not as scientific as in-person or phone surveys that use a random sampling of the population, online surveys are a low-cost way to do market research about whether an idea or a product will be appealing to consumers. Now many companies offer to conduct online research for you or give your company the tools to carry out your own surveying. Some online survey companies includeEZquestionnaire, KeySurvey, and WebSurveyor.

Research Tools and Techniques

There are a variety of types of market research tools -- both offline and online -- that are used by many large businesses and can be available to small and mid-sized businesses. When these techniques involve people, researchers use questionnaires administered in written form or person-to-person, either by personal or telephone interview, or increasingly online. Questionnaires may be closed-end or open-ended. The first type provides users choices to a question ("excellent," "good," "fair") whereas open-ended surveys solicit spontaneous reactions and capture these as given. Focus groups are a kind of opinion-solicitation but without a questionnaire; people interact with products, messages, or images and discuss them. Observers evaluate what they hear.

Major categories are as follows:

1. Audience Research. Audience research is aimed at discovering who is listening, watching, or reading radio, TV, and print media respectively. Such studies in part profile the audience and in part determine the popularity of the medium or portions of it.

2. Product Research. Product tests, of course, directly relate to use of the product. Good examples are tasting tests used to pick the most popular flavors—and consumer tests of vehicle

or device prototypes to uncover problematical features or designs.

3. Brand Analysis. Brand research has similar profiling features ("Who uses this brand?") and also aims at identifying the reasons for brand loyalty or fickleness.

4. Psychological Profiling. Psychological profiling aims at construction profiles of customers by temperament, lifestyle, income, and other factors and tying such types to consumption patterns and media patronage.

5. Scanner Research. Scanner research uses checkout counter scans of transactions to develop patterns for all manner of end uses, including stocking, of course. From a marketing point of view, scans can also help users track the success of coupons and to establish linkages between products.

6. Database Research. Also known as database "mining," this form of research attempts to exploit all kinds of data on hand on customers—which frequently have other revealing aspects. Purchase records, for example, can reveal the buying habits of different income groups—the income classification of accounts taking place by census tract matching. Data on average income by census tract can be obtained from the Bureau of the Census.

7. Post-sale or Consumer Satisfaction Research. Post-consumer surveys are familiar to many consumers from telephone calls that follow having a car serviced or calling help-lines for computer- or Internet-related problems. In part such surveys are intended to determine if the customer was satisfied. In part

this additional attention is intended also to build good will and word-of-mouth advertising for the service provider.

Writing Online Questionnaires

When it comes to using Web-based surveys, small businesses should stick to a few simple but important rules:

• The Shorter the Better. Don't alienate survey takers with long questionnaires. Limit yourself to 25 questions, which should take people five to seven minutes to finish, says Mary Malaszek, owner of Market Directions, a Boston market-research firm that works with businesses of all sizes. If surveys are much longer, people will abandon them 'and then you can't use them, and the next time you send them a survey they won't even open it,' she says. Other methods for keeping surveys short, according to a SensorPro white paper on online survey guidelines: make the first page simple, present answer options in multiple columns or a drop-down box, and put a status bar at the top of each question page so respondents know how close they are to being finished.

• Avoid Open-Ended Questions. Since people want to zip through a survey, don't include a lot of open-ended questions where they have to type out the answers. Close-ended questions they can click on a button to answer—Yes, No, Maybe, Never, Often—work much better, Malaszek says. Companies can use close-ended questions to get the same kind of in-depth analysis open-ended questions provide by using rankings scales, which ask a respondent to rate something on some type of scale, 1 to 5, or 1 to 10, she says.

• Be Persistent. If you're asking customers or vendors to take a survey, it's okay to send more than one invitation, especially to people who've previously indicated they would be willing to participate. Just make sure you've got people's permission, so they don't think you're spamming them, the survey experts say.

• Be Patient. Businesses decide they want to do a survey then get impatient when they can't get the results right away, Malaszek says. Even though online surveys reduce some of the work, they take time to design and administer, and when the results are in, more time to interpret. It's a good idea to pick one person to shepherd the process, she says.

Bibliography

Brown, Damon. "Using the Web for Market Research." IncTechnology.com, October, 2006.

Clegg, Alicia. "Market Research: Through the looking glass."Marketing Week. 16 March 2006.

Mariampolski, Hy. Qualitative Market Research: A Comprehensive Guide. Sage Publications, 21 August 2001.

McQuarrie, Edward F. The Market Research Toolbox: A Concise Guide for Beginners. Sage Publications, 15 June 2005.

The Five Basic Methods of Market Research

While there are many ways to perform market research, most businesses use one or more of five basic methods: surveys, focus groups, personal interviews, observation, and field trials. The type of data you need and how much money you're willing to spend will determine which techniques you choose for your business.

1. Surveys. With concise and straightforward questionnaires, you can analyze a sample group that represents your target market. The larger the sample, the more reliable your results will be.

• In-person surveys are one-on-one interviews typically conducted in high-traffic locations such as shopping malls. They allow you to present people with samples of products, packaging, or advertising and gather immediate feedback. In-person surveys can generate response rates of more than 90 percent, but they are costly. With the time and labor involved, the tab for an in-person survey can run as high as $100 per interview.

• Telephone surveys are less expensive than in-person surveys, but costlier than mail. However, due to consumer resistance to relentless telemarketing, convincing people to participate in phonesurveys has grown increasingly difficult. Telephone surveys generally yield response rates of 50 to 60 percent.

• Mail surveys are a relatively inexpensive way to reach a broad audience. They're much cheaper than in-person and phone surveys, but they only generate response rates of 3 percent to 15 percent. Despite the low return, mail surveys remain a cost-effective choice for small businesses.

• Online surveys usually generate unpredictable response rates and unreliable data, because you have no control over the pool of respondents. But an online survey is a simple, inexpensive way to collect anecdotal evidence and gather customer opinions and preferences.

2. Focus groups. In focus groups, a moderator uses a scripted series of questions or topics to lead a discussion among a group of people. These sessions take place at neutral locations, usually at facilities with videotaping equipment and an observation room with one-way mirrors. A focus group usually lasts one to two hours, and it takes at least three groups to get balanced results.

3. Personal interviews. Like focus groups, personal interviews include unstructured, open-ended questions. They usually last for about an hour and are typically recorded.

Focus groups and personal interviews provide more subjective data than surveys. The results are not statistically reliable, which means that they usually don't represent a large enough segment of the population. Nevertheless, focus groups and interviews yield valuable insights into customer attitudes and are excellent ways to uncover issues related to new products or service development.

4. Observation. Individual responses to surveys and focus groups are sometimes at odds with people's actual behavior. When you observe consumers in action by videotaping them in stores, at work, or at home, you can observe how they buy or use a product. This gives you a more accurate picture of customers' usage habits and shopping patterns.

5. Field trials. Placing a new product in selected stores to test customer response under real-life selling conditions can help you make product modifications, adjust prices, or improve packaging. Small business owners should try to establish rapport with local store owners and Web sites that can help them test their products.

12

Public and press relations

What is PR?

Every organisation, no matter how large or small, ultimately depends on its reputation for survival and success.

Customers, suppliers, employees, investors, journalists and regulators can have a powerful impact. They all have an opinion about the organisations they come into contact with - whether good or bad, right or wrong. These perceptions will drive their decisions about whether they want to work with, shop with and support these organisations.

In today's competitive market, reputation can be a company's biggest asset – the thing that makes you stand out from the crowd and gives you a competitive edge. Effective PR can help manage reputation by communicating and building good relationships with all organisation stakeholders.

Our definition of Public Relations:

Public Relations is about reputation - the result of what you do, what you say and what others say about you.

Public Relations is the discipline which looks after reputation, with the aim of earning understanding and support and influencing opinion and behaviour. It is the planned and sustained effort to establish and maintain goodwill and mutual understanding between an organisation and its publics.

Terms

The following terms are used in the definition of PR:

• 'Organisation' can be a government body, a business, a profession, a public service or a body concerned with health, culture, education - indeed any corporate or voluntary body large or small.

• 'Publics' are audiences that are important to the organisation. They include customers - existing and potential; employees and management; investors; media; government; suppliers; opinion-formers.

• 'Understanding' is a two-way process. To be effective, an organisation needs to listen to the opinions of those with whom it deals and not solely provide information. Issuing a barrage of propaganda is not enough in today's open society.

http://www.cipr.co.uk/content/careers-cpd/careers-pr/what-pr

8 principles of effective public relations

The NonProfit Times

Getting good press coverage used to be referred to as "good ink." That saying seems a little quaint now, with even major magazines like Newsweek going online only. But, having a good public relations strategy for the media is still important for nonprofits.

David Fenton and Lisa Chen, two executives at New York City-based Fenton, wrote in the book "Nonprofit Management 101" that the basics of getting attention for your cause are the same even though people get a lot of their news online. Those eight principles are:

• Principle #1 – Tell Unforgettable Stories: Make your story "sticky," that is, make it something people want to read. That means it needs to include distinct characters.

• Principle #2 – Meet People Where They Are – Then Bring Them Along: Before you can take people where you want them to go on your issue, you have to find common ground with them.

• Principle #3 – Repeat Yourself: You must design scenarios that repeat the story many times in many different venues.

• Principle #4 – Build Relationships of Trust with Reporters: As MSNBC's Chris Matthews once put it, "It's not who you know. It's who you get to know."

• Principle #5 – Simplify Your Issue: "Simple" does not mean dumbing down – just the opposite. Simple is smart because it means more people will understand why your cause is so important and be inspired to act.

• Principle #6 – Harness Influential Messengers: Sometimes the messenger is as important as the message.

• Principle #7 – Use Advertising to Make News: With the right combination of bold strategy and media outreach, it's possible to parlay a modest ad buy into millions in free, "earned media."

• Principle #8 – Don't Let the Opposition Control the Conversation: Hunkering down and hoping that negative publicity will simply go away is never a good PR strategy.

http://www.thenonprofittimes.com/management-tips/8-principles-of-effective-public-relations/

How to: write the perfect press release for journalists

Laura Oliver

Journalism.co.uk asked its readers what they want - and what they don't - from a release

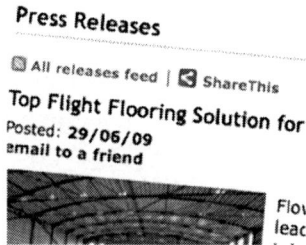

Whether you think there's a better alternative or you'd rather receive PR pitches by Twitter, press releases are still a popular format for public relations and communications teams when contacting journalists.

But how can these releases become as popular with the journalists receiving and reading them?

To help improve our own press release service, PressGo, for both press release posters and journalist users,Journalism. co.uk asked for your advice on writing the perfect press release.

Below is our crowdsourced guide, broken down into sections corresponding to different aspects of a release and with the contributors name in brackets.

You can jump to different sections using the links below and feel free to add more pointers in the comment box:

Before you write the release:

• If the PR in question has time, have a quick look at the site they are pitching to, to get an idea of the tone of writing and the type of article that does well. Use this to make the press release a bit more relevant. (Rebecca Thomson, reporter, computer Weekly)

• Provide clear relevance to my 'beat'. I hate it when I am the recipient of scattered buckshot that has no relevance for my publication but I have to plough through a lot of information before I realise this. (Gillian McAinsh, La Femme editor, The Herald, South Africa)

• Ask yourself these three questions:

1. Is your press release really necessary?

2. If you were running a story based on this release, what would be the headline be and does the first sentence fit into less than 15 words? If no, or the first sentence is 'Mrs Miggins plc announces...', go back to Q1.

3. If you got Q2 right, why are you changing the wording for a press release? (Chris Edwards, freelance journalist)

Format

• Don't send the release as attachment only. A release under the phrase 'Press release, see attached' and no other details is likely to be deleted with extreme prejudice and the company added to a spam list. (Mark Robertson, journalist/producer, BBC Cumbria)

• Send a pretty PDF of the release to your client if you must, but send copy to journalists as plain text. PDFs and other formats often add weird character breaks and slow down the editing process. (Carlton Reid, editor of bikebiz.com)

Headlines

• Headlines should be as short and interesting as possible. (Rebecca Thomson, reporter, Computer Weekly, UK)

• A headline should be short enough for a Twitter update including a link. (Sarah Taylor, Inspiring Communication)

• If you're emailing the press release, you've only got a handful of words in the subject line to grab journalists' attention and if the first four are 'Press release: Market leading...' chances are you're not going to get many hacks to actually read the rest of the subject line, let alone open the email/release itself. (Journalism.co.uk blog commenter 'Hack')

• The headline should clearly contain the value of the press release to the reader. It should not contain the name of the issuing organisation -for example: 'NPR announces new special initiative' - obviously it's NPR, they're sending the press release. (Matt Forsythe, social media manager, National Film Board of Canada)

Subject matter and language

• I get loads of press releases that are boring and paragraphs or even sentences containing lots of technical terms make me want to break things. Reporters get told to constantly ask the question when thinking of stories, 'why would people care about this?'. I think PRs should ask themselves that question when writing releases. (Rebecca Thomson, reporter, Computer Weekly, UK)

• Press release writers should make it clear why my readers need to know about their product. That is, provide a news angle to their releases. (Gillian McAinsh, La Femme editor, The Herald, South Africa)

• The biggest bugbear with press releases I find is the vague, nonsensical terms - leading, highly scaleable, holistic, end to end solution etc. Please, tell us in as plain a language as you can, what your client and their product does. (Journalism. co.uk blog commenter 'Hack')

• My personal peeve is when press releases make tenuous, unbelievable tie-ins to current topics to get attention. Bad form. (Phill Dolby, freelance journalist)

• Purge superlatives. (Carlton Reid, editor of Bikebiz.com)

Summaries

• Bullet points at the top, summarising the main points, are helpful. (Rebecca Thomson, reporter, Computer Weekly, UK)

• If you have to distribute a release that has already been approved by a US client, try rewriting the first paragraph as a 'news in brief' item and put that in the email before the press release. If you can condense your story into a NIB and save journalists some time, then it's more likely to be used. (Journalism.co.uk blog commenter 'Josie', referencing advice from social media consultant Nick Booth)

• Summaries of the organisation's history or relevance are not required. A single line to tell us who you are is enough. (Matt Forsythe, social media manager, National Film Board of Canada)

Paragraph structure

• Summarise what you are selling early on in the release, preferably using the standard journalism 25 words of 'who, what, where, when, why'. Releases often lack the time and place of an event, which can make all the difference. (Gillian McAinsh, La Femme editor, The Herald, South Africa)

• Don't bury any, 'actually, the study doesn't really show what the title of this press release says it does' content down toward the bottom. (Journalism.co.uk blog reader 'Anna')

• Once you've written your press release, go away and make a coffee. Come back and notice that the whole point of the release is in the last paragraph. This is because you were thinking to A4 scale and after writing seven paragraphs of waffle you had a space of one-paragraph left in which to squeeze your essential. Now make the last paragraph your introduction and go and have a second well-deserved coffee. It's a cliche, but the sting is often in the tail. (Tony Trainor, freelance journalist)

Length

• Never, ever, write more than two pages - preferably one. (Sarah Taylor, Inspiring Communication)

• Two-hundred-and-fifty words is enough to say everything. Add a link to a longer post if there are specific details that need to be added. (Matt Forsythe, social media manager, National Film Board of Canada)

Quotes

• Only include a quote that someone might actually have said. No 'strategic partnership solutions' language (anywhere, but particularly not in the quote). (Sarah Taylor, Inspiring Communication)

• Please don't quote people who aren't available for interview - there's nothing more annoying than getting a release and then finding the subject isn't available to talk. (Journalism.co.uk blog reader 'Hack')

Case studies

• Please stop sending me case studies. I don't care what Wigan Council has done with its IT support, unless it's moved its server to the moon or something. (Rebecca Thomson, reporter, Computer Weekly, UK)

Images

Some differing opinions from our participants about the best way to handle images:

• Fancy graphics or big pictures just fill up my inbox, meaning I might have to delete the release without really reading it. If I want pictures I'll ask for them, and graphics might look nice but they're just annoying to someone who gets hundreds of (uninteresting) emails each day. The release needs to be really easy to scan quickly and graphics can get in the way. (Rebecca Thomson, reporter, Computer Weekly, UK)

But if images are really an essential part of what your release is about:

• Supply clear, usable photographs. (Gillian McAinsh, La Femme editor, The Herald, South Africa)

• Always include two or three pictures in the actual release rather than fob people off to a website where they then have to spend ages finding images that you [the press release writer] should have found for them. (Journalism.co.uk blog reader 'Kate')

Contact details

• Don't send out a release and then go on holiday for two weeks the next day. It's amazing how often this happens. It's very annoying if you need to speak to the author urgently. (Journalism.co.uk blog reader 'Kate')

• Always put your phone number somewhere instead of hiding behind an email address. There isn't always time for email queries. (Journalism.co.uk blog reader 'Kate')

http://www.journalism.co.uk/skills/how-to-write-the-perfect-press-release-for-journalists/s7/a535287/

13

<u>Customer Relationship Marketing (CRM)</u>

The Business Case for Building Real Relationships with Customers

Given the wealth of information available online, relationship marketing is becoming ever more important.

Why? Because today's consumers are more informed than you can imagine. This has resulted in a drastic shift in consumer power and has altered the selling process by placing a greater emphasis on the customer experience.

Most businesses do not have a clear understanding of what relationship marketing really is and how to successfully put it into practice. Let's debunk one misconception right from the start: Relationship marketing isn't the opposite of traditional marketing and it doesn't exclude older channels (like email marketing and content marketing) in favor of solely using social media.

To clarify this important practice, today we'll look at the most important online channels in relationship marketing campaigns. We'll even give you the inside scoop from notable entrepreneurs on how relationships helped build the audiences that built their businesses.

Let's jump in!

What is Relationship Marketing Really About?

With a focus on loyalty, retention and long-term relationships, the aptly named practice of "relationship marketing" is designed around developing strong connections with customers by directly providing them with information that is tailored to their needs, wants and interests.

As opposed to transactional marketing's focus on direct sales, relationship marketing emphasizes increased word-of-mouth activity, repeat business and a willingness on the customer's part to provide information to the organization. And unlike "interruption" marketing, this process is started willingly via an opt-in by the customer.

But is this focus on creating a relationship with customers worthwhile? As we previously discussed, the shocking truth of brand loyalty is that most customersdonot want to be engaged with a business or brand; their priority is shared values.

The secret here is that the relationship marketing process has nothing to do with engagement and everything to do with being practically useful for both your business and customers.

According to a management study by Robin Buchanan and Crawford Gillies, the increased profitability associated with relationship marketing is the result of several factors:

• There's less "dating around." Satisfied, long-term customers in your marketing funnel are statistically less likely to switch. As an added bonus, they tend to be less price-sensitive; experts say that customers who feel taken care of are less concerned about what they are paying.

FACT: relationship marketing is effective in stopping customers from "dating around" with the competition. http://hlp.sc/12rbbzs

• It's the foundation of word of mouth. Strong relationships are essential to a high net promoter score, or, in other words, the chance that a customer will happily refer your business to a friend.

Research shows that relationship marketing can improve your Net Promoter Score. http://hlp.sc/12rbbzs

• Your "regulars" are your rock. Regular customers tend to buy more often and they are less expensive to maintain because of their familiarity with your business and the processes behind it.

Consumer data reveals that regular customers spend more and are less expensive to maintain. http://hlp.sc/12rbbzs

• Expansion becomes easier. Longstanding customers are much more likely to purchase your ancillary products and embrace your new ventures (think of those folks you know who buy each new Apple gadget).

A recent study has shown that having long standing customers makes business expansion less risky. http://hlp.sc/12rbbzs

• You avoid the cost of acquisition. The famous Bain & Company analysis that it is 6 to 7 times more expensive to acquire a new customer than to keep a current one is something that keeps marketers up at night, but businesses with high rates of customer satisfaction needn't worry about high churn rates.

Did you know that relationship marketing helps lower the cost of acquisition AND increase retention? http://hlp.sc/12rbbzs

There were also some less-obvious benefits noted in the study, such as the fact that companies with strong loyalty measurements tend to be far more capable of shutting out new competitors and generally don't have to worry about competing products (as much).

Lastly, companies with superior loyalty metrics make their employees' jobs easier and more satisfying, resulting in a less-stressed and more competent workforce (this one surprised me!).

The bottom line: For customers who do want a relationship with your brand, their concerns are primarily about how useful you prove yourself to be (outside of your product).

Relationship marketing through these channels ...

• Customer service

• Content

• Social media

• Email

• Loyalty programs

• Surveys

...is the ticket to earning your way into their good graces. Your reward for these efforts, as noted in the research above, is being able to build a company that customers love to talk about.

Below, let's take a look at how your business can use these individual channels. Take note of the practical advice from entrepreneurs who have placed a priority on building great customer relationships and have been amply rewarded for their efforts.

1. Customer Service

No matter how high tech customer relationship management becomes, the high-touch elements of personal support will always be the foundation great customer service is built on. The cornerstones for providing memorable customer support are reciprocity and personalization. To achieve these ends, it's imperative to create a balance that provides employees with clear goals and guidelines (but doesn't suffocate them with red tape!).

To help you get started, we recommend you read the following (free) guides:

Remember that the companies who truly lead the way in exceptional service have this goal ingrained in their culture, so make sure you take the time to invest in employees who get why it's important to take care of customers.

2. Content

"What if businesses decided to inform, rather than promote? You know that expression 'If you give a man a fish, you feed him for a day; if you teach a man to fish, you feed him for a lifetime?' The same is true for marketing: If you sell something, you make a customer today; if you help someone, you make a customer for life. In every business category, one company will commit to being the best teacher, and the most helpful. And that company

will be rewarded with attention, sales, loyalty and advocacy by consumers who are sick to death of being sold, sold, sold."

Jay Baer, author of Youtility

Content marketing is such a hot topic right now that calling it a hot topic has become a trope in itself!

But there's a reason for this. Traditional paid advertising—the standard interruption marketing method—essentially amounts to renting eyeballs or clicks for your business. Once the money stops flowing into those channels, the results also stop.

By contrast, content marketing allows you to build an audience that you can keep. It should not be viewed as a traditional marketing expense since the returns for evergreen content will last as long as the thoughts stay relevant.

But content goes far beyond acquisition. Using content as a form of support is also marketing. Free resources, help documentation and webinars can marketing to customers (as Des Traynor notes here) as long as the content is:

• Functional

• Comprehensible

- Usable

- Enjoyable

- Motivational

We love this graphic on content marketing from our friends at Intercom:

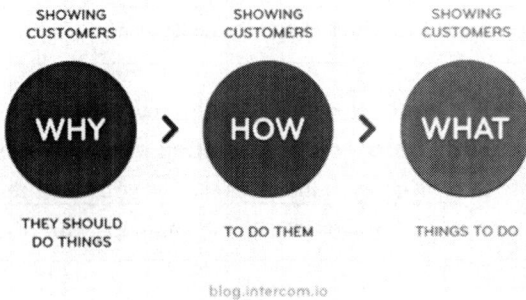

Is your content doing all of the above? If not, it's time to rethink your execution.

3. Social Media

If you can get past the hype, social media can truly be a useful channel for creating relationships with customers.

There are multiple approaches to using social media to build relationships, all of which need to properly reflect your brand's values. As an example, see how FedEx has used social media to build trust and prestige with customers and to successfully resolve issues:

Even though FedEx does online listening, Sauerwein's team is the one responsible for handling actionable requests that customer care follow-up to help solve the issue or answer the question. Their engagement time?Mostly in a matter of minutes."

Conversely, brands like Taco Bell who, let's be honest, aren't catering to a professional B2B audience, focus more on connecting with customers through humor. The result: Their Twitter account has become one of the most popular online corporate accounts.

Patrick Saleeby @littleepistles   13h
If Taco Bell thinks they're revolutionary by putting nachos inside of a burrito, then they've never met a drunk person.
Expand

TACO BELL @TacoBell   10h
@littleepistles Where do you think we got the idea?
Hide conversation   Reply   Retweet   Favorited

1
FAVORITE

1:24 AM - 6 Jun 12 via Twitter for iPhone · Details

Building relationships through social media is about knowing who your audience isand creating a social media presence that reflects what they want to see from you. If you've earned the right to appear in their streams, keep it by giving them content that they actually want.

4. Email

"Email marketing is still one of the most powerful mediums to build relationships with your customers, as it is just so personal. At work, many employees spend 2 ½ hours in their inbox—that's a lot of time! Incorporate this channel by delivering free course content and product updates via email. A consistent stream of genuinely useful content will guarantee that your campaign is really effective—and it's something that business owners have never been able to deliver over display ads or social networks."

Chris Hexton, co-founder of Vero

There's a reason every social network in existence asks for your email when you sign up: Email is still the best way to turn a casual browser into a repeat user, and there's a plethora of data to back that statement up.

ROI

Email:	$40	for every $1 spent
Keyword ads:	$17	for every $1 spent
Banner ads:	$2	for every $1 spent

Email marketing for small businesses thrives off of an engaged email list resulting from strong relationships being built with customers and prospects.

One benefit of email that isn't often mentioned is that you rarely have to compete with fun via email. On Facebook during the summertime I wish your updates and ads the best of luck, because you'll be competing with BBQs and bikini photos and they likely won't stand a chance.

What's the point in creating useful resources for customers if they never hear about them? Having a clear, distraction-free channel to notify customers of these offerings is how you can elicit responses like this:

The takeaway: Don't let your updates get drowned in a sea of nonsense. Build relationships by getting customers to opt-in for email updates.

5. Loyalty programs

Creating "sticky" customer loyalty programs is no easy task, but successful programs show that it's more than worth the effort.

As with every aspect of relationship marketing, creating a great loyalty program starts with knowing what your customers want and what they want to do in order to get it (oftentimes this is simply buying more of your products, which is great!).

Here's a quick 3-step rundown of how to angle any loyalty program toward customers' needs:

1. Find a desirable outcome. Customers won't commit to a program if the reward isn't worthwhile. Additional access or bonuses for your product may be the way to go, but in many cases free stuff works best.

2. Find an action they will regularly commit to. Dropbox found that customers were very willing to refer other users for additional space. For other businesses (like the car wash example), simply purchasing the product or service will be enough (i.e., rewarded for buying something they already want).

3. Make sure this system aligns with your business. With business goals in mind, the loyalty program should be crafted around your business' modus operandi.

A slightly crazy example of the last tip can be found in loyalty programs from companies like Neiman Marcus:

"Committed customers, however, spend from $75,000 to just under $600,000 a year just to earn access to concierge service, private off-hours shopping events, custom travel and a whopping 5 points per dollar spent. For the Chairman's Circle members who spend more than $600,000 a year at Neiman's or Bergdorf Goodman, it's unparalleled access to a store they're practically living in anyway."

This program may seem insane to the average business, but when you are a luxury brand like Neiman Marcus and your customers regularly reach such numbers, it just makes sense!

6. Surveys

Most people don't understand that building a relationship with customers is about helping them. I've learned that the best way to find out how to help is by using surveys. By regularly using both standard surveys and targeted micro-surveys, we've gained a deep understanding of what customers want. We've even gathered feedback for non-product related concerns, such as what content customers would find most useful."

Ruben Gamez, founder of Bidsketch

Customers are far more willing to hand over information to companies they know, like, and trust ... and the data gathered can be incredibly valuable to your business.

Of the many methods to gather feedback from customers, surveys offer the best way to approach customers on a large scale. As Gamez mentions above, surveys can be useful to gather a sense of a majority opinion for an upcoming decision (like what sort of content customers might enjoy most).

We've previously written an entire post on creating smarter customer surveys, so I'll spare you the tactical information on what gets surveys completed. But make sure you're familiar with the three things every survey should be laser-focused on:

1. Intent. Why are we making this survey? What do we want to learn?

2. Brevity. Is this question really necessary?

3. Bias. Is this a loaded question? Are we communicating clearly with customers?

When you conduct smart, regular surveys with your customers (and prospects), you'll take a lot of the guesswork away and end up with insightful data that you can use to evaluate your next move.

14

EXPERIENTIAL MARKETING

What is Experiential Marketing?

Attack! Marketing September 23, 2013

Experiential Marketing

Experiential marketing is a form of advertising that focuses primarily on helping consumers experience a brand.

While traditional advertising (radio, print, television) verbally and visually communicates the brand and product benefits, experiential marketing tries to immerse the consumers within the product by engaging as many other human senses as possible. In this way, experiential marketing can encompass a variety of other marketing strategies from individual sampling to large-scale guerrilla marketing.

In the end, the goal of experiential marketing is to form a memorable and emotional connection between the consumer and the brand so that it may generate customer loyalty and influence purchase decision.

History and Development:

As B. Joseph Pine II and James H. state in their book, The Experience Economy, the number of goods and services has increased making the industry as a whole increasingly competitive and crowded. They illustrate that brands must begin to provide consumers with memorable events and engagements that allow the brand to stand out from the clutter of their competitors. Livy Alvey, in Relationship Marketing, explains further that brands facing identical competitor products can create brand loyalty by focusing on the emotional connection.

Marketing Strategies that go into Experiential Marketing:

Brands utilize a variety of marketing strategies in order to achieve this emotional connection with their consumers. When it comes to which marketing strategies to use, it depends more on how they are used, the target demographic of the product, and the emotion that the brand wants to associate with itself.

On July 10th, Adidas organized the "D Rose Jump Store" in London to promote Derrick Rose's signature Adidas sneakers. Although the concept was simple (use Derrick Rose's presence to create buzz among fans), Adidas took it to another level by adding depth to their activation. In addition to meeting the famous Chicago Bulls point guard, fans had the opportunity to win a free pair of the signature sneaker if they could jump 10 feet to reach them. By having participants jump the same distance needed to reach a regulation basketball hoop, it gave each consumer perspective into the basketball player's life. Whether participants walked away empty handed or with a new $100 set of shoes, they all had an experience that they will always remember and associate with Adidas.

For some brands, a custom made store that is only open for one day is unnecessary to experience their product. Landshark Lager is confident that in the right setting, there is nothing better than their American lager. So on October 7th, the brewery targeted popular pools in the Las Vegas area and provided free samples of their beer. Landshark capitalized on the refreshing feeling of going to the pool on a warm day to communicate that their beers can be just as refreshing. Landshark was able to create an experience for their consumers with a relatively inexpensive and straightforward distribution strategy.

When Brands Use Experiential Marketing

Brands most often use experiential marketing either to enhance and complement a traditional advertising campaign or to stand out at a popular event or conference. However, as honest internet virality gains more and more influence, many brands have begun executing experiential marketing campaigns that exist on their own.

To bolster a television spot that AdWeek described as "mediocre", Coca-Cola organized an experiential marketing activation in which consumers take on the role of a Double O agent and sprint through a train station. After purchasing a Coke Zero, the vending machine challenged drinkers to reach another section of the train station, weaving through preplanned obstacles, in order to receive free tickets to the newest Bond film, Skyfall. In addition to giving each participant a Bond-like experience they will never forget, an edited taping of those participants went viral (currently sporting over ten million views).

A more endearing example of experiential marketing, and one that illustrates a campaign that stands on its own, is one recently activated by Milka. The chocolate brand made the effort to manufacture 10 million bars that were missing one piece. Puzzled chocolate eaters then learned that the one piece had been set aside for them to choose whether they would want it mailed back to them or mailed, with a personalized message, to a friend or loved one. This campaign helps the brand not only form an emotional connection with its consumer, but also to whomever the consumers decides to send the single piece of chocolate to.

http://www.creativeguerrillamarketing.com/guerrilla-marketing/experiential-101-experiential-marketing/

Experiential marketing is here to stay

Chris Russell, managing director, Tribe

The best agencies are true experience-makers which bring brands to life. And consumers love it. So in today's economy, experiential marketing is even more relevant, writes Tribe's Chris Russell.

Sponsored by Tribe

What's your view of experiential marketing? Ten years ago, for most marketers, it was just about getting the brand out there by handing out samples and promotional vouchers, or pulling off stunts that got people talking about brands. Today, it's about creating memorable experiences for consumers and giving them the chance to really interact with a brand.

With so much economic uncertainty, today's consumers are more cautious, so brands need to assess how consumers respond to different marketing channels. From what we're seeing at Tribe – particularly in the results of a white paper we recently produced – this means experiential marketing is going to become an increasingly important way for brands to engage with consumers.

Chris Russell, managing director, Tribe

What do consumers respond to?

We carried out two surveys at the beginning and end of 2012. These gave us a chance to see how the economic downturn is affecting consumers' attitudes to different marketing channels, which ones they respond to most and which ones would make them more likely to buy a product.

The results show that well over half of the 1,100 consumers we asked say they prefer experiential to every other form of marketing. In particular, it matches up very strongly against press and radio. But it is even preferred to other forms such as TV, which has a far longer shelf life.

The surveys also show that in today's economic climate, consumers place increasing importance on product samples and reduced price offers as an introduction to brands. In fact,

48 per cent say they are more likely to buy a new product if they can try it first.

Experiential marketing also scores highly in encouraging more purchases from existing customers, attracting lapsed customers and inspiring repeat purchases.

Overall, according to our findings, experiential marketing increases overall and spontaneous brand awareness, purchases and recommendations by more than 50 per cent. So, if brands are assessing the effectiveness of their marketing channels, then they should be considering experiential.

The pop-up Eurostar experience was taken to cities outside of London

Bringing brands to life

But experiential marketing is about more than just giving consumers samples and offers. It's also about delivering a live brand experience that engages them and encourages them to interact with the brand. And our survey shows that it's far more effective than any other channel in engaging consumers. Over 50 per cent of people say they spend between one and

10 minutes a day engaged with a brand through experiential marketing, compared with less than a minute through TV and Facebook.

To make the most of this consumer engagement, the challenge for experiential marketing agencies is to become true experience-makers. What does that mean? For us at Tribe, it's about understanding you as marketers, your brand challenges and your audience. And then it's about developing great creative ideas that wow consumers both online and offline.

Particularly in today's economic climate, when consumers are cautious, we believe that to bring brands to life you need to go beyond representing them as merely an ambassador.

Instead, we're developing a group of people who know brands inside out, are passionate about them and who are prepared to fight to give them the exposure they deserve. We call them 'brand warriors'.

Brand warriors

Brand warrior training programmes help maximise immediate sales

The people who are out on the streets representing your brands need to be as immersed in, knowledgeable about and passionate about your brand as you are.

To be a brand warrior you need to understand the product as well as the guy who made it. Or sell it like the people in the brand's flagship store. And be able to identify the most likely customers and spend more time engaging with them.

But you still need the personality to involve consumers in a conversation, excite them about the brand and create a real connection that generates sales.

Our brand warriors understand that consumers value experiential as a way of discovering and developing loyalty for a brand. And they make sure that the brand experiences they create are more focused, more enjoyable and, ultimately, more valuable.

Initiation

To develop these brand warriors requires a change in the way they're recruited, trained and developed. So, there are no more X-Factor-style auditions where everyone gets the chance to do their party piece.

Instead, we've developed a rigorous initiation process, designed to identify the very best people.

We choose them based on their ability to fight for your brands. And once they've passed this initiation, we train them thoroughly in the brands they'll be representing. So, once they get out on the streets, in stores and at events, they're fully immersed in your brand.

And they come from a variety of backgrounds – from nutritionists and vets to actors, singers and dancers.

Alesha Dixon appeared at the grand opening of a Best Buy store

But first and foremost, they need the passion and drive to be a brand warrior.

An essential tool

So, experiential marketing is a highly professional and relevant sector that focuses on targeting the right audiences in the right way. And, as our survey results show, brands should be using it as an essential marketing channel. In fact, experiential should be at the forefront of every brand's creative thinking.

It's a growing professional sector that's proving itself for brands time and time again. And, just as importantly, experiential marketing is the channel that resonates stronger with consumers than any other. Not only do consumers enjoy the experiences it offers, but it's delivering real value and better return on investment for brands than it ever has.

And now, with brand warriors fighting for your brands, you know that you're being represented by people who are as excited about your brands as you are. And you can be confident that experiential marketing will be one of the most effective weapons in your marketing armoury for years to come.

http://www.marketingweek.co.uk/analysis/supplements/ agency-opinions-field-and-experiential-marketing/experiential-marketing-is-here-to-stay/4005877.article

15

Online/Digital Marketing

How to Get More Visitors to Click, Buy or Promote on Your Site

Dave Lavinsky

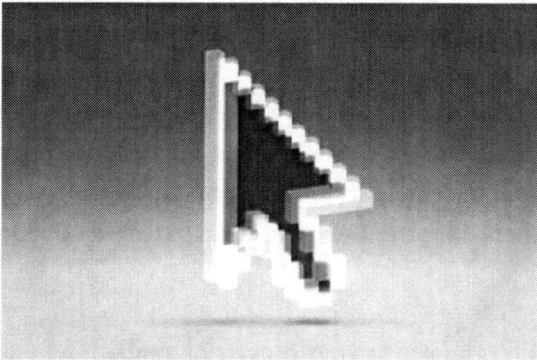

Image credit: Shutterstock

If you're wondering whether your website is good enough, I'll give you the answer: No, it's not.

How can I be so sure? Because every website can be improved. There is no website in existence where 100 percent of the visitors take the precise action the website owner wants. Which means there's always room for improvement.

This leads to the next logical question of how to improve your website. To answer this, start by figuring out the primary goal of your page. Is it to generate online sales, get prospects to complete a form, encourage visitors to call you or get folks to click to promote your site on social media?

Related: Bring Traffic to Your Site With These 4 Blogging Alternatives

Once you understand your goal, work backwards. That is, think about the path through which visitors must travel to achieve this goal. For example, if you sell one product on your website, the desired path for visitors to take might be to visit your homepage, click your product sales page to learn more about your offering, click the order button to get to your order form, then complete the order form to arrive at your thank you page.

This path is known as your conversion funnel, and the key to success is to improve or optimize every piece of the funnel. For example, let's assume that on your website 30 percent of visitors to your homepage then go to your product sales page. Twenty percent of those visitors proceed to your order form. Finally, 40 percent of the remaining visitors complete the order and arrive on your thank you page. In this case, 2.4 percent of all visitors completed the funnel, also known as a 2.4 percent conversion rate.

The key to improving your conversion rate, and the success of your website, is to improve each page in your conversion funnel. In fact, if you increased the conversion rate of each page in your funnel by 10 percent, then your overall conversion rate grows a whopping 33 percent.

Related: All Content Isn't Created Equal: Tips For Making Yours Top-Notch

Unfortunately, most entrepreneurs and business owners fail to measure their website's conversion rates. Even when they do, most inevitably only look at their overall conversion rate. Rather, the key is to assess the conversion rate of each page in your funnel. Then improve those pages and see exponential increases in your overall conversion rates.

How do you increase the conversion rate of each page? There are many factors to consider and ideas to try, from changing your choice of text, modifying text size and/or font choice, adding new images, modifying your layout and changing the background color of your page.

Importantly, track the conversion rate of each of your pages both daily and monthly. On a daily basis, your rates might fluctuate quite a bit due to small sample sizes. When viewing your results on a daily basis, make sure there are no dramatic conversion drops which are often caused by a page, image or video not loading. And importantly, make sure your pages are improving daily. On a monthly basis, see how your pages are performing and spot which ones are decreasing in effectiveness and thus need to be improved.

In summary, it's the individual pages in your website's conversion funnel that determine whether your website performs well or not. Fortunately, if you monitor and improve these pages, you will convert significantly more website visitors into leads and clients, and gain significant competitive advantage.

http://www.entrepreneur.com/article/231530

Search Engine optimization

SEO Tips and Tricks for 2014

Search Engine Optimization in 2014 is too complex for beginners so they must need to follow some Best SEO Tips and Tricks that will boost their Website ranking better in modern Search Engines.

So here we are going to see some Basic and Intermediate SEO Tips and Tricks that helps to improve your website ranking in Search Engine Results Page.

Most of bloggers using Wordpress so we recommend to use top wordpress SEO Plugins

Tips and Techniques for Keyword Analysis

The Below list will help to improve the Keyword Analysis better.

1. Use Google Keyword Planner

2. Find Less Competitive Keywords with high search Volume

3. Choose Key phrases

4. List out Relative Keywords by relevance

Google Keyword Planner - Google Keyword Planner is the free SEO tool that is provided by Google and it helps to find out the Keywords search volume and relative Keyword ideas for you. Useful tool compare with other keyword analysis tool because Google is the top Search Engine used by people so it's worth to use this tool. See this 8 Free Google SEO Tools that help to Optimize your website

Less Competitive Keyword with high Search Volume - Finding this one is crucial part of SEO because if you find out this Keyword then you can get high search visitors. More competitor's means ranking high is also too much tough. So find out less completive Keywords.

Choose Key Phrases - Rather than selecting a single Keyword it's better chance to ranking more than one keyword if you chosen Key Phrases. So select Key phrases that works better compare to keywords.

Excellent SEO Tips to improve On-Page optimization

1. Interesting and Descriptive to read

2. Quality of the Content

3. Short and Sweet Title

4. Relative Meta Description

5. Optimal Keyword Density Ratio

6. SEO Friendly Url

7. Keywords in First Paragraph

8. Use of Headings

9. Focusing Keywords

10. Image Optimization

Interesting and Descriptive article - No one is going to like boring long articles so write your content interest to read and descriptive content that will clear all things about the article title.

Quality of the Content - Don't copy Paste whole content from the other website that never going to bring you traffic. Google has very good eye to find out the Duplicate contents. Avoid Keyword stuffing and other Black-hat SEO tricks.

Shot and Sweet Title - Title must be relative and the Key phrase Keywords must be present in the Title. And in length is better to keep it between 40 to 65 Characters. And read more Tips to Title Tag Optimization.

Relative Meta Description - Writ a short and sweet 156 Characters that will explain your whole story of the article will help to know better in Search Engines Results Page.

Optimal Keyword Density Ratio - Maintain your Keyword Density in the Safe manner to not getting Google Algorithm Penalties.

SEO Friendly URL - Url of the content must be meaning full to the content. Then search Engine highlight the Url Keywords also it's a boosting signal for the SEO.

Keyword in First Paragraph - Use the Keywords in First Paragraph so search Engines know this is the content really explains about the Title.

Use of Headings - Use prober headings tags h1, h2, etc... It will make readability easier and Nice Chapter wise content.

Focusing Keywords - Highlighting the Keyword with strong or em tag will increase the visibility of the point you are really want to reader by people also it's add some weight in SEO.

Image Optimization - One Image can explain everything better than long story content so add an image and Optimize image using proper Alt Tags.

Tips to improve Off-Page SEO

1. Use of Social Media

2. Quality Link Building

Use of Social Media - Use of Social Media not going to build follow back links but it's a powerful source to deliver traffic to the website. Traffic signal is also important factor in SEO so use the social media to get traffic.

Quality Link Building - Don't build your Link too much faster. Quantity of Back links that's not matter Quality will Matter. So write your articles good and interesting then the Back link will flow automatically to your content.

Useful SEO Tricks for 2014

1. Find LSI Keywords

2. Use LSI Keywords more

3. SEO Check Up

Find LSI Keywords - Find the Latent Semantic Indexing Keywords related to your keywords using different methods available in the internet.

Use LSI Keywords more - Rather than Keyword stuffing the new idea use mixes it up LSI Keywords with Keywords as Keyword Stuffing. Use it in all important On-Page SEO Factors.

SEO Check Up - Take SEO Check Up and using different tools available in the Internet and improve the SEO Score by fixing by the tips then you can get a better rank in SERP.

Add a Bookmark of this Page above Tricks will be updated in regular manner to maintain the Quality of the Article.

Necessaries of SEO Tips and Tricks in 2014

Competitive world everything will have some Guidelines and rules that must we need to follow. So we need to follow this techniques to survive our ranking in search Engines.

Always one thing we need to remember in SEO that is if we write Unique and Good Articles that is interest to read for a user not for search engines this is the one rule always survives you in SERP.

Hope this SEO Tips and Tricks will helps to boost your rank in Google in 2014.

http://www.bestseoideas.com/best-practices/seo-tips-and-tricks-for-2014

5 SEO Techniques You Should Stop Using Immediately

Neil Patel

When you're doing your site's SEO, you have to be careful. The techniques that used to work will now get you penalized. The techniques that used to be a waste of time are now indispensable.

Now and then, we need to be reminded what works and what doesn't. As it stands today, there are five SEO techniques that I need to warn you about. These techniques could be hurting your site.

Technique #1: Spammy Guest Blogging

Earlier this year, Matt Cutts came out with an announcement that sent tremors through the web community:

If you're using guest blogging as a way to gain links in 2014, you should probably stop.

Here's what happened after he published that blog post: Mayhem. Unleashed.

Guest blogging has been a pillar of content strategists and SEOs for a long time. Was Cutts really pulling the plug on the practice?

Yes and no.

The fact is not a single line of algorithmic code was changed when Cutts clicked "publish" on his post. The panic was overrated. The people whoshould be scared are the people who are sending emails to me and Cutts asking for guest posts so they can pop in a backlink.

That's why Cutts rattled his saber against guest blogging. The spammy SEOs had once again twisted a good thing — guest blogging — into a black hat technique.

There is legitimate guest blogging, and then there is spammy guest blogging. I'm a major fan of guest blogging, and I still recommend that you practice it, but with caution.

Since guest blogging got the hairy eyeball from Cutts, I think the algorithm will shift to start suppressing spammy guest blogging results. Here's what the change might look like:

• First, Google will crack down on guest post links that are irrelevant to the site's theme. For example, you think an auto insurance sales links on forbes.com/technology is a good idea? Not going to happen.

• Second, Google will tighten the penalties on optimized anchors in guest posts. Optimized anchors are always bad, but it's likely that the penalties will be swifter and harsher on those that appear in guest blogs.

• Third, Google will increase the algorithmic importance of Google authorship and authority. This is a critical determining factor already. It's important to keep a pulse on it. In order to look at your own metrics, go to Google Webmaster Tools > Labs > Author Stats. Your personal authority as an author will have an increasing importance upon the validity of your guest blogging.

And if you're doing any of the following with your guest blogging, I recommend that you stop.

• Using optimized anchors (more on that below) in your guest posts

• Attempting to rank for long tail keywords in your guest posts

• Attempting to rank for head terms in your guest posts

• Writing irrelevant content in your guest posts

• Writing low-quality content in your guest posts

Right now, guest blogging is still a viable option for improving SEO, enhancing brand awareness, and even building your author rank. However, you need to be extremely careful how you execute your guest blogging plan.

Bottom line: Use guest blogging with caution.

Technique #2: Optimized Anchors

For a long time, SEOs used anchor texts with keywords to improve their SEO. The great thing was it worked! But the days of optimized anchors are gone. Today, using optimized anchors is like asking for a penalty.

So what's an optimized anchor? An optimized anchor is an anchor text that uses keywords for which you want to rank. For example, if a site wants to rank for the term "top mobile phone," it would use the anchor "top mobile phone" to link to its mobile phone site.

It worked great until Google warned against this practice in its "Link Scheme" document.

The text reads:

Here are a few common examples of unnatural links that may violate our guidelines…

Links with optimized anchor text in articles or press releases distributed on other sites. For example:

There are many wedding rings on the market. If you want to have awedding, you will have to pick the best ring. You will also need tobuy flowers and a wedding dress.

In other words, don't optimize anchor texts. I've seen optimized anchor texts ruin a site's SEO through gradual algorithmic penalization. The best I can say about it is that it's extremely risky.

I know what you are thinking, "Well, what kind of anchors do I use?"

That's a great question. There are several types of safe anchors that I recommend:

• Naked URLs like this one: www.quicksprout.com

• Branded URLs like this one: For more advice on content marketing, check Quicksprout.

• Long phrases like this one: I'm a major fan of guest blogging, andI still recommend that you practice it with caution.

Links are still important, but their SEO value has more to do with their mere existence than it does with their anchor text.

Bottom line: Use safe anchors, not optimized anchors.

Technique #3: Quantity of links over quality

The more backlinks your site gets, the better, right?

No.

Purchasing backlinks is quick, easy, and pretty cheap. You can find any number of SEO agencies who will build a bunch of links for you. In the course of a week or two, they can pile up a few dozen links pointing directly at the pages you specify.

But that could ruin your site, especially if the following is true:

• The site that links is penalized.

• The site that links has a low DA (e.g. below DA 20).

• You receive a large number of such links in a short period of time.

Link building has been and still is the bread and butter of many SEO agencies. However, any SEO value from link building depends upon the authority and validity of the site that is sending the links.

Here's a quick example. I watched this site languish under a shoddy SEO campaign for months. The SEOs employed by the company were drumming up quick and easy links like crazy. It hurt. Then, when they engaged in an aggressive content marketing campaign with an SEO upside, things changed:

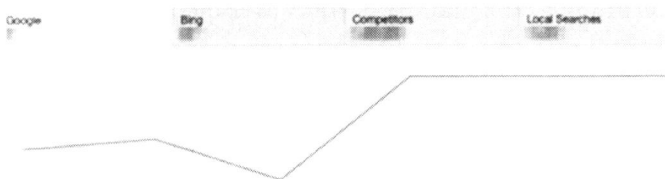

The uptick coincided with a very small number of high-DA backlinks (2 DA 90+ links). The decline coincided with the deluge of low DA backlinks.

Bottom line: Link building is still alive and well, but don't try to do it with lots of low-DA backlinks. There is a better way.

Technique #4: Keyword Heavy Content

It's old news that keyword stuffing is bad. This is one of the earliest tricks in the SEO playbook.

Here's how Google defines keyword stuffing:

"Keyword stuffing" refers to the practice of loading a webpage with keywords or numbers in an attempt to manipulate a site's ranking in Google search results. Often these keywords appear in a list or group, or out of context (not as natural prose). Filling pages with keywords or numbers results in a negative user experience, and can harm your site's ranking. Focus on creating useful, information-rich content that uses keywords appropriately and in context.

In spite of the of warnings and consequences of keyword stuffing, I still see it happen.

Here is how Matt Cutts, in a 2011 video, illustrated the effect of adding more and more keywords. Up – plateau – down.

It's like a bell curve. Add a keyword or two, and you'll gain some rank. Keep adding keywords, and it doesn't really add much rank benefit. Keep adding keywords, and you'll start to lose rank.

In other words, keyword stuff and get penalized.

I want to add something new to this discussion rather than just give you the same worn out warnings. Here are four pieces of advice that will help you avoid keyword-heavy content and produce penalty-free content.

• The kind of keyword stuffing that gets penalized is long tail keywords rather than head terms. For example, "San Francisco hotel vacation cheap" is a long tail keyword. Drop that in your content a few too many times, and a penalty isn't far behind. However, if you have to use the term "San Francisco" quite a few times, that's okay.

• Add more content, not just more keywords. The most important thing about keywords is not how many times they occur. I recommend adding more content — both the number of posts and the length of that content. The more pages you have, the more pages on your site will be indexed. When you have lengthy and substantial content on those pages, you'll have more reader-focused material and related terms.

• Don't worry about keyword density. Instead, worry about creating really good content for your readers. There was a time when "keyword density" was a big deal. In fact, many SEO writers actually had to run keyword density analyses on their content to make sure that they were in the correct density percentage range. Your goal instead is to shape content for your readers, not the search engines.

• Use related keywords. There's been some confusion (and change) over the use of latent semantic indexing (LSI) with Google. Whatever Google's current use of LSI, keep in mind that related keywords are important for both avoiding keyword stuffing and improving your search results. For example, instead of using "San Francisco hotel vacation cheap" a dozen times, you would include natural phrases like "places to stay in the Bay Area" or "lodging near Union Square."

Bottom line: Go easy on the long tail keywords. Instead, publish more articles with longer content.

Technique #5: Relying on link-backs instead of content

Link-backs, while important, are not the only component of SEO. There is a delusion that merely throwing a lot of links to a site will magically bring massive authority, high rankings, and tons of search traffic.

That's simply not the case.

Truly effective SEO is about the sum of several parts — not one or two techniques pushed to the extreme.

Think about SEO as if it were a fork. A fork doesn't work if it has just a single tine. A one-tine fork is a spear. A two-tine fork doesn't work either. Effective forks have several tines — usually four.

SEO is the same way. In order to be effective, you have to use all four components of SEO:

Links are just part of the solution, not the whole thing. You can rack up a huge link profile, but unless you're advancing your efforts with content marketing, social signals, and solid onsite optimizing (site speed, UI, etc.), you're wasting your time and money.

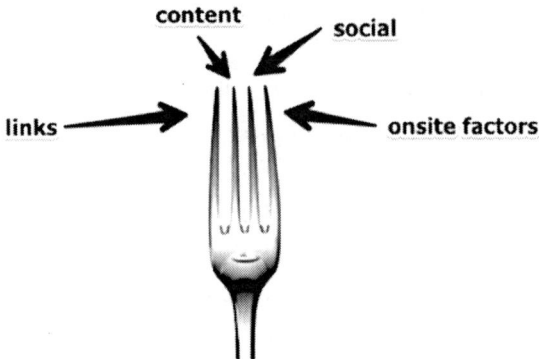

Bottom line: Use a link-back strategy, but keep it balanced with the entire suite of SEO — content marketing, social media, and onsite optimization.

Conclusion

SEO isn't about the latest tricks or techniques. It's a long-term strategy that takes into account all relevant factors.

This article provides some much-needed warnings. It's time to back off the gimmicks that you thought would work. SEO is not dead, but it has changed. You need to adapt your strategy accordingly.

What is pay-per-click advertising?

Joanne Jeffs

Using PPC advertising you can quickly make your business website visible in the search engines and to start generating traffic.

You may have heard about pay-per-click advertising which is also referred to as PPC, search engine marketing (SEM), keyword advertising or paid search. I still find it a challenge to explain exactly what PPC advertising is despite working in PPC Management for over five years. This is because there are so many interpretations and misconceptions floating around.

This form of online advertising is still seen as an alien concept. I think this mainly due to the fact that unlike traditional forms of advertising such as TV, newspapers and radio most people have a limited understanding of how it works. So here is a top level explanation:

Online advertising

PPC advertising is a form of online advertising that is used to increase the number of people visiting your website. Lots of businesses have identified the need to have a website, so they spend a lot of time and money to produce a well-structured, designed and search engine optimised (SEO) website.

Then work doesn't stop there, however. You need to make sure your site can be found and encourage potential customers to visit your website.

The solution is PPC advertising. It is the perfect method of online advertising to quickly make your site visible in search engines, and to start generating traffic to your site.

Where can I see examples of PPC?

The most common form of PPC ads are displayed on search engine results pages (SERPs) above and to the right-hand side of the organic results in response to the users search term. They are clearly labelled as 'Ads' or 'Sponsored Results' to differentiate them from the organic listings.

The image above shows the difference between PPC ads and organic listings for a Google results page.

PPC advertising is very flexible and quick to set up in comparison to other types of online advertising.

http://business.hibu.co.uk/knowledge/articles/2011/sept/what-is-payperclick-advertising/

How to Use Google AdWords

Use Google AdWords Effectively

Understanding how to use Google AdWords is vital to your online marketingefforts, with AdWords being the most popular form of pay-per-click (PPC) marketing.

Using AdWords enables you to advertise on Google, the most popular search engine, which in turn enables you to get your advertisements in front of the biggest potential audience.

How To Use Google AdWords : Tips, Tools, And Resources

Creating and optimizing campaigns for AdWords can be difficult, but the benefits are tremendous. WordStream offers a number of tools and resources for business and agencies looking to improve their campaigns and learn how to use Google AdWords effectively. Whether you are an AdWords novice picking up a copy ofAdWords for Dummies, or a PPC expert looking to advertise on Google, we have the resources for you.

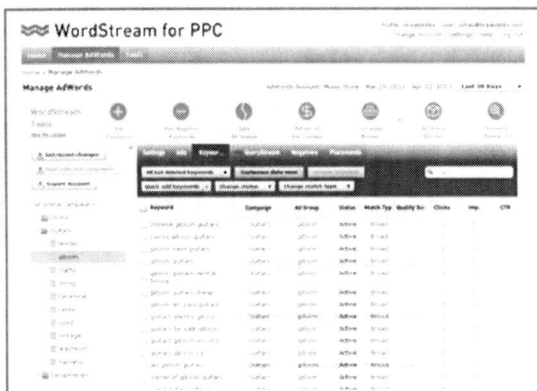

Webinars – Watch our past Google AdWords webinars online, download the slides, or sign up for our next upcoming marketing webinar!

AdWords Ebooks Collection – Browse through our large assortment of AdWords EBooks, covering everything from using Negative Keywords, improving Quality Score, to selecting different AdWords match type options.

Free AdWords Performance Grader – The grader evaluates your Google AdWords account based on important metrics like Quality Score, click-through-rate, and long-tail keyword optimization. You'll get actionable tips on how to improve your score and optimize your campaigns immediately.

Learn How to Use Google AdWords from the Experts – Read our collection of interviews with PPC experts who scored unusually high on our AdWords Performance Grader and offered to share their AdWords secrets for Google AdWords success.

Subscribe to the WordStream Blog – Our award-winning blog is constantly updated with new tips and guides for PPC marketing. Learn all about how to use Google AdWords.

Free Keyword Tools – Use our collection of free keyword tools to optimize your AdWords campaign! The collection of free keyword tools includes:

• Free Keyword Tool

• Free Keyword Niche Finder

• Free Keyword Grouper

• Free Negative Keyword Tool

Try Wordstream for PPC Free! - WordStream offers powerful PPC solutions that can help you succeed when you use Google AdWords. Our robust software takes you through all the steps to create and optimize your campaigns.

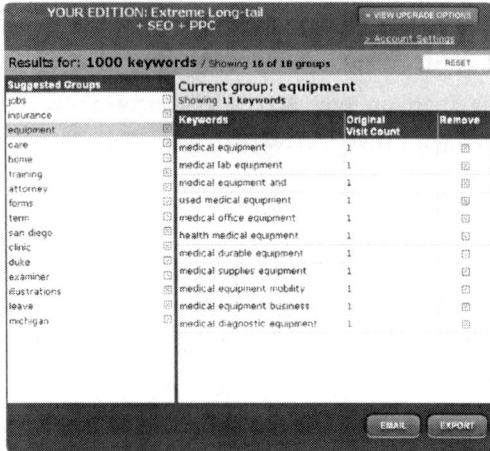

How To Use Google AdWords : Buying Keywords On Google

AdWords is Google's pay-per-click (PPC) advertising platform and its main source of revenue. In the AdWords paid search advertising model, advertisers can bid on the keywords they want to trigger their sponsored ads that appear in the search engine results page (SERP). When you use Google AdWords, Google decides which ads are displayed and in what position based on each user's maximum bid and Quality Score.

Quality Score is determined by a number of factors:

• Relevance of ad copy

• Relevance of the ad to its corresponding landing page

• The ad's click-through rate (CTR)

• Historical account performance

• Other relevance and performance factors

The single most important factor in using Google AdWords effectively is relevance.

Why is relevance so important?

Google want to connect searchers with advertisements that match their search query and help them find what they are searching for. Google rewards advertisers who have tight, relevant groupings with higher Quality Score.

A higher Quality Score gives advertisers better AdWords ad positions, and more impressions as a result. Improved Quality Score also lowers your cost-per-click (CPC), making it a key factor to focus on.

You can improve your Quality Score by implementing a focus on relevance into you campaigns. This means having relevance:

• Between text-ads and your keywords

• Among the keywords in each of your ad groups

• Between your advertisement and its corresponding landing page

A higher Quality Score equates to more impressions at lower costs, lowering your cost per click and cost per action.

This might seem like a lot to keep track of, but search advertising on Google AdWords doesn't have to be overwhelming. WordStream's PPC management system is a unique tool specifically designed to help advertisers use Google AdWords effectively through simplifying and improving the PPC marketing processes so that you can maintain high Quality Scores and collect search-driven profits. WordStream offers all the assistance you need to learn how to use Google AdWords.

WordStream also offers online marketing services for web marketers looking to hand over their PPC accounts to Google AdWords experts.

How To Use Google AdWords : Keyword Discovery And Grouping

Before you can have relevance between your keywords, you need to first generate a list of keywords for your Google AdWords campaign. Brainstorming your business's keywords can be a huge hassle, which is why WordStream offers a free keyword generator tool to help you through the process. While you could use the Google keyword tool to begin your keyword research, it's inherently limited. When you use the Google AdWords keyword tool, you get results based on global search data, not on the effectiveness of these terms as directly applied to your website.

WordStream's Keyword Research Suite gives you deep access to WordStream's industry-leading, trillion-keyword database, giving you the competitive edge of knowing your keywords are more extensive and accurate.

Once you have your keyword list, you'll want to segment your keywords into manageable, tightly related groups. It can be daunting to look at extensive keyword lists and try to determine the optimal number of keyword groups and how to create keyword groups for maximum relevance. But it's essential to do this-- forming well-structured ad groups is a key component in learning how to use Google AdWords effectively. Our free keyword grouper tool can help make this process easy.

How To Use Google AdWords : Writing Clickable Text Ads

When you are creating ad text, you want your ads to have a clear, compelling message. Make sure your ad is relevant to your keyword and landing page, and be sure to include a call to action as well!

WordStream's PPC Management software includes ad-text generation tools that will help you attract the prospective customers you're after while raising your CTR and Quality Score.The text ad generator tool automatically populates the fields of your Google ad with the most popular and relevant keywords in your ad group, helping you hone in on keywords and phrases that will appeal to your potential customers.

How To Use Google AdWords : Let WordStream Help

In addition to our cutting-edge WordStream for PPC Software, WordStream also offers comprehensive Managed Services in which our Google Certified AdWords Experts help craft, manage, and maintain your Google AdWords account so that it is always in peak performance.

http://www.wordstream.com/how-to-use-google-adwords

16

Marketing Media

Creating a Media Plan

The standard media plan covers four stages: stating media objectives, evaluating media, selecting and implementing choices, and determining the budget.

KEY POINTS

• Media objectives are normally stated in terms of three dimensions.

• There are definite inherent strengths and weaknesses associated with each medium so many advertisers rely heavily on the research findings provided by the medium, by their own experience, and by subjective appraisal when deciding which media to use.

• The media planner must make media mix decisions and timing directions, both of which are restricted by the available budget.

When choosing the media, you not only need to know which media outletsexist, but also which ones suit your product. You probably will not want to contact local business publications if you want to advertise the authors and schedule of the new reading program you are creating. However, if you want to focus on the support of the business community in pulling this off, then this is exactly who you would want to contact.

Developing the Media Plan

Advertising media selection is the process of choosing the most cost-effective media for advertising to achieve the required coverage and number of exposures in a target audience.

Although the media plan is placed later in this process, it is in fact developed simultaneously with the creative strategy. This area of advertising has gone through tremendous changes; a critical media revolution has taken place.

The standard media plan covers four stages: (a) stating media objectives; (b) evaluating media; (c) selecting and implementing media choices; and (d) determining the media budget.

Stating Media Objectives

Media objectives are normally stated in terms of three dimensions:

1. Reach: The number of different persons or households exposed to a particular media vehicle or media schedule at least once during a specified time period.

2. Frequency: The number of times within a given time period that a consumer is exposed to a message.

3. Continuity: The timing of media assertions (e.g., 10% in September, 20% in October, 20% in November, 40% in December and 10% the rest of the year).

Evaluating Media

There are definite inherent strengths and weaknesses associated with each medium. In addition, it would require extensive primary research, either by the sponsoring firm or their advertising agency in order to assess how a particular message and the target audience would relate to a given medium. As a result, many advertisers rely heavily on the research findings provided by the medium, by their own experience, and by subjective appraisal.

Selection and Implementation

The media planner must make media mix decisions and timing directions, both of which are restricted by the available budget. The media mix decision involves putting media together in the most effective manner. This is a difficult task and necessitates quantitatively and qualitatively evaluating each medium andcombination thereof.

Unfortunately, there are very few valid rules of thumb to guide this process, and the supporting research is spotty at best. For example, in attempting to compare audiences of various media, we find that A C Nielsen measures audiences based on TV viewer reports of the programs watched, while outdoor audience exposure estimates are based on counts of the number of automobile vehicles that pass particular outdoor poster locations.

The timing of media refers to the actual placement of advertisements during the time periods that are most appropriate, given the selected media objectives. It includes not only the scheduling of advertisements but also the size and position of the advertisement.

Setting the Media Budget

The media budget is a subset of the advertising budget, and the same methods used to create advertising budget will be used to create the media budget.

In general, remember that:

• Media outlets which deliver messages involving multiple senses (sight, sound, touch, and smell) will be more expensive than those involving just one sense (sound).

• The quality expectations of the media outlet will influence the cost. For example, the quality of ads for national television stations tend to be higher than those for local outlets. Creating a text ad on the Internet, however, can be free or cost next to nothing.

https://www.boundless.com/marketing/advertising-and-public-relations/the-advertising-campaign/create-a-media-plan/

Your Social Media Marketing Plan in 5 Easy Steps

Jasmine Sandler

This solid, measurable plan (along with a commitment to developing consistent and valuable content) will help you drive online brand awareness, customer engagement, and audience growth.

Many marketers launch their social media programs because they feel they need to and then scramble to understand both how they will make these work and how they will be managed. Most of them do this with no goal in mind and worse, no understanding of how social media marketing (SMM) works.

Many believe that social is the answer to customer acquisition and are short-sided in defining realistic results. Unfortunately this all results in lost time, lost customers, lost market share, and lost profitability.

Stop chasing your tail in social. Start your SMM planning right by following these five easy steps.

SMM Step 1: Create Your Executive Overview Business Plan

Spell out your business in a one-pager to realize why you need social:

• Your Business Mission and History

• Your Business or Revenue Model

• Descriptions of your Products & Services

• Details of Your Target Audience

• Review of Your Current Marketing Efforts

SMM Step 2: Define Your Specific Social Media Goals

It is impossible to reach and attain a goal without defining exact specifics. Too many business owners let social metrics define their goals, such as "More Twitter Followers", "More Fans on Facebook", "More YouTube Views."

As marketers, we all know that it is really about engagement that counts. But, what engagement are we talking about? Positive engagement?Volume of commenting on a controversial piece of content?

You need to go a step beyond to define specific, actionable, and (most importantly) reasonable SMM goals. Here are some specific SMM goals you might use after completing your business review:

• Validate a new product or service using social as a research platform.

• Develop buzz and interest around a new product.

• Engage users in social to generate relevant and targeted traffic to your site.

• Gain market share by leading customer/client service through social.

• Generate registrations to branded events through social.

SMM Step 3: Find Your SMM Voice

One of the keys to ensuring your success in social is to create and implement a voice that resonates with your specific target audience. For each audience type, break down and research age, income, location, and reasons for possibly buying your products/services.

SMM Step 4: Choosing Your Social Tools Appropriately

Choosing your social tools appropriately is an essential piece of your online communications plan, so choose wisely. Let's do a short review of the leading social sites to assist you in your selection:

• Facebook:More than 955 million users. Majority between 18-25; 60 percent female. Best opportunity for community building with customers.

• Twitter:More than 555 million users. Majority between 26-34; 57 percent female. Best tool for interacting in real-time.

• Google Plus+:More than 170 million users. Majority between 26-34; 63 percent male. Platform for driving visibility around a brand.

• LinkedIn:More than 150 million users. Majority between 26-34, directly followed by 35-44. The number one B2B social networking tool.

• Pinterest: More than 12 Million Users. Majority between 26-44; 68 percent female. A viral platform for sharing stories via pictures.

SMM Step 5: Plan & Execute Content & Delivery

Now to the hard part – finding, creating, and delivering engaging social media content. Social media execution can be daunting, but with a proper plan it is doable and can drive real (marketing) results.

What you need to define:

• Your frequency of content delivery & response to social engagement.

• Your types and specific topics for content creation.

• Ways to increase audience engagement.

• Events that can drive social.

• Your social success metrics (number of followers, number of fans, volume of traffic back to site, number of retweets, etc.).

Summary

Social media marketing can be an excellent vehicle for developing online brand awareness, customer engagement, and audience growth. This requires a solid, measurable plan and a commitment to developing consistent and valuable content. In addition, it's crucial for you to have a clear understanding of why social can be useful for reaching your business goals.

http://www.clickz.com/clickz/column/2203265/your-social-media-marketing-plan-in-5-easy-steps

17

THE FUTURE OF MARKETING

5 Predictions On The Future Of Marketing, PR and Advertising Agencies

Unless you are petting fluffy bunny in the forest and didn't get the memo, it is no secret that the world of marketing, PR and advertising is changing at lightning speed.

It used to be that things were neatly divided into pretty categories:

An advertising agency created ads (and if they did media placement, they placed the ads). Some of course were better than others.

A marketing agency could do a variety of things depending on their specialty ranging from brand identity (design, slogan, etc.), perhaps creating your website, some paid advertising (overlaps a bit with an advertising firm), maybe helped with events and other ways to get the word out (such as digital fun things like search engine optimization or more traditional like direct mail). Some of course were better than others.

A public relations agency focuses on media attention. This used to be limited to pitching traditional media for articles, placement, etc. Some firms helped you put on events. Some of course were better than others.

And in each category of course, there are consultants that help clients DIT: Do It Themselves.

And then the social and creative web started to become mainstream and the game has completely changed. Things are smarter, faster, cheaper as opposed to dumber, slower, expensive.

The happy divide between marketing, advertising and public relations has crumbled.

Now there amazing do-it-yourself tools that entrepreneurs, big brands and all clients can use if they so choose.

Many companies (big and small) can handle all their marketing, public relations and advertising themselves (this wasn't true even just ten years ago).

However, There will always be a market though for those that need some help. They just might not need help from a bloated agency using old-school tactics (that was said nicely wasn't it)?

Now, many firms, consultants, etc. are re-branding. Perhaps they are now communications companies, or social media marketing companies (yikes), digital marketing agencies, we-make-you-money-hahaha companies, buzzword-of-the-day firms or whatever. Evolution is good for those that understand how to maximize the new (and ridiculously changing world). Evolution is bad for the ones sitting there yearning for the days of yesterday.

Plus, client expectation and education levels have changed. Folks have become (and continue to be) much more educated on things like social media, blogs, search engine optimization and creating online content.

Which leads to this question: What is the future of marketing, PR and advertising agencies going to look like?

While I don't have a crystal ball (or do I? muhahaha) based on thousands of conversations with entrepreneurs, big brands, consultants and agencies, and through content consulting here are some thoughts:

1. Jacks Of One Trade: Specialized Experts

The days of Mad Men are long gone. Bloated agencies are screwed. Why? For one thing: MASSIVE overhead. Big buildings, segways for employees, whatever.

This model ends up driving up expense and instead of a well oiled machine, creates an environment that often isn't cutting edge, but slow-moving. Slow to make decisions. Slow to take action. I know I'd rather work with a lean agency with a specific specialization than a "jack of all trades that costs me my first born."

Sure, it is nice to have "everyone under one roof" for control purposes, but now there is this Internet thing and more ways to do work virtually. A team of freelancers can be assembled in a jiffy. Or a consultant. Does it take more work on the agency end to do this? Absolutely. But why hire a bunch of experts as opposed to bring them in on a per project basis or set up a referral network?

I'd bet the future will be more about partnerships between highly specialized experts as opposed to the big box model.

2. Help With Content

It used to be that if you had a budget, you could just hand over all of your marketing, advertising or public relations and sit back and "watch and approve the magic." The problem with this, and where we are going in the future, is that smarter, faster, cheaper promotion and advertising requires participation from the client.

Because smarter, faster, cheaper is all about the client becoming a trusted resource as opposed to a product pusher. The go-to person. Online and off.

New marketing isn't about banner ads or a firm "Tweeting and interacting online on behalf of you", it is about content. Let's pretend your client is "Joe's Delicious Dog Food."

Perhaps you help Joe create "The Dog Hour" an online show or podcast. Or a doggy get-together where people bring out their pets. Or "Doginars" where Joe helps teach old dogs new tricks (couldn't resist).

Joe is the thought leader. He knows the content. You don't. But, you can help if you have a knowledge of what kind of content spreads, how to create it, market it, measure it and monetize it.

There is a huge value to help clients with this and agencies of the future are going to have to hop onto the content train. Toot.

3. Agencies Become Educators

Teaching will be another model that will continue to take shape. More specifically, teaching people and companies. Not keeping the secret sauce secret. This means educating and enabling as opposed to controlling (practice what you preach, right?).

This means agencies/consultants, etc. will continue to create their own content online and off.

Perhaps it is monthly events in your home town where you invite out business owners and marketers.

And in many ways, this content can be monetized directly. Perhaps instead of clients, you have subscribers and create a community. A membership site or a mentoring program.

The end result is part publisher and part agency.

4. Not Outsourcing Relationships

Let's talk about social media for a second. A lot of agencies and consultants are offering social media services for their clients. Great.

But, what exactly is being offered and what should be offered?

Can an agency assist with content creation? Can an agency find relevant articles/other content in your niche to share on Twitter, Facebook, etc.? Can an agency suggest people to follow? Can an agency set up a Facebook page and Twitter account for you? Can an agency suggest tweeting topics? Can an agency post content to your Twitter and Facebook accounts? Suggest blogs and forums you should be participating in/on? I would say YES to all of the above with millage varying.

But can an agency "be you" and act like you online? Form relationships with people? Small talk and make it look like it is coming from the CEO? The answer here is a resounding NO.

If a goal is to build relationships and trust, you can't outsource it. The client HAS to participate. This doesn't mean sitting behind the computer all day, but it does mean dedicating some time to interacting which is social aspect of social media.

The problem we all see over and over is an agency doing all of the above in the YES category and ignoring the NO category or trying to it themselves. This is sure recipe for disaster and either results in a broadcast stream (aka a bullhorn with no interaction) or fake interaction done by the agency as opposed to the person (the human) that needs to be doing it. Yuck.

As with everything, time to evolve.

5. Respect The Blogger And New Media Sources

I'm not suggesting that traditional media is dead. It isn't. I'm not saying traditional advertising is dead. It isn't. But, there are some incredible opportunities online to generate buzz, sales, trust and more that many agencies aren't educated on.

There are blogs and new media sources with incredible sponsorship and advertising opportunities that go beyond print ads, 30-second ads and the dreaded banner ad (more on this in an upcoming post). Not only are they cost-efficient, but they laser cut the demographic you are looking for.

In our example, "Joe's Delicious Dog Food" in the past might be "pitched" by an agency to the local paper. 93% of the readers couldn't care less about dogs (probably more). Or perhaps the agency places one of Joe's commercials on Animal Planet. Good choice, but still not a guarantee that people watching a lion eat a duck (or something) own a dog. Plus, I bet that ad is super expensive.

As opposed to pitching the local paper, why not start building relationships with bloggers and new sources in your clients niches? Keyword here is relationships (In many cases traditional and new media are different animals. Different etiquette. Different wants and needs. Trust me.)

Why not help Joe form a relationship with 20 dog bloggers? Perhaps Joe can guest post on their sites and Joe can put up their blogs on his website. Or he can give them some dog food to try and ask for an honest review.

Or on the paid side, why not sponsor a doggy web show or podcast? I bet it will cost a FRACTION of a TV ad, reach dog owners and allow more bang for the buck. Perhaps Joe goes on the dog show to talk about nutrition for animals. Or the trusted show hosts plugs the food. Or Joe sponsors a series called "Getting Doggy With It" where the show host records doggy karaoke. OK, I'm getting nutty here, but you get the idea.

Traditional media in many cases is like a one night stand. It is hot, sexy and then it is over. Online media (content sponsorships, guest posts on blogs, blurbs, etc.) is more like a long-term relationship. Online content is spreadable and can increase in value over time since is stays up.

Agencies of the future will have to learn a little more respect for the blogger and new media source.

Wrapping It Up:

All in all, these are VERY exciting times for both agencies, consultants, business owners, entrepreneurs, marketers looking to evolve and maximize the newest era of business.

Some will be left in the dust of course, but many will thrive.

http://www.therisetothetop.com/davids-blog/5-predictions-future-marketing-pr-advertising-agencies/

Lightning Source UK Ltd.
Milton Keynes UK
UKOW04f0042240614

233938UK00017B/965/P